OF HUMANS, PIGS, AND SOULS

HAU
Books

ESSAYS IN ETHNOGRAPHIC THEORY

The ethnographic essay provides a creative form for new work in anthropology. Longer than a journal article, shorter than a conventional monograph, ethnographic essays are experiments in anthropological thought, probing particular cases, topics, or arguments, to propose in-depth but concentrated analyses with unusual insight. In the past these were often published by research institutes or academic departments, but in recent years the style has enjoyed less space than it deserves. HAU Books is pleased to offer room for renewing the essay as an anthropological genre. Our Essays in Ethnographic Theory are published as short books, in print, ebook, and open-access PDF editions.

OF HUMANS, PIGS, AND SOULS

An Essay on the Yagwoia *Womba* Complex

Jadran Mimica

Hau Books
Chicago

ISBN: 978-1-912808-31-1 [paperback]
ISBN: 978-1-912808-71-7 [ebook]
ISBN: 978-1-912808-35-9 [PDF]
LCCN: 2020950104

Hau Books
Chicago Distribution Center
11030 S. Langley
Chicago, Il 60628
www.haubooks.org

Hau Books is printed, marketed, and distributed by The University of Chicago Press.
www.press.uchicago.edu

Printed in the United States of America on acid-free paper.

In loving memory of my friend

James "Jimmy" Weiner/Jaimie Pearl Bloom

1950–2020

Contents

List of Figures

Acknowledgments

I am grateful to the Yagwoia people with whom I forged that unique bond of friendship, empathy, and love which only the pursuit of ethnographic knowing and its correlative transformation into anthropological gnosis can bring into existence. Among so many irreplaceable Yagwoia men, women, and children of all ages, through whom I got to know them and their life-world, I will mention by their endearment names (*ilaye yeuwye*) the following five: *Hiwoye, Hitane, Qwa:ce-ungwaṯanye, Wopaye*, and *Kaṯace*.

Regarding my anthropological colleagues, I thank the members of the departmental seminars at the University of Sydney, Macquarie University, and the University of St. Andrews where I presented several short versions of this study.

I also thank Gillian Gillison for her insightful comments on an early version of this essay.

I owe special debts to the former editor of HAU Books, Giovanni de Col, who, having read my first submission intended as a longer paper, suggested that I expand it into a monograph. Subsequently, Hylton White made invaluable editorial comments which, together with the reports by two anonymous reviewers, enabled me to transform the manuscript into its present form. In this regard, my special thanks to Caroline Jeannerat, who copy-edited the manuscript.

I am also grateful to my wife, Ute Eickelkamp, for her comments that greatly enhanced the overall textual flow.

Finally, I thank Taylor & Francis Publishers for letting me reuse my chapter published in the volume *Psychoanalysis and other matters: Where are we now?*, edited by Judith Edwards (London: Routledge, 2019).

List of abbreviations

PNG   Papua New Guinea
SDA   Seventh-Day Adventists

Kinship terms

B	brother
Ch	child/children
D	daughter
F	father
G	grand-kin
GF	grandfather
H	husband
M	mother
S	son
Z	sister
1S	first person singular
3S	third person singular

Other terms

∧   simultaneous relation of conjunction and disjunction

Map

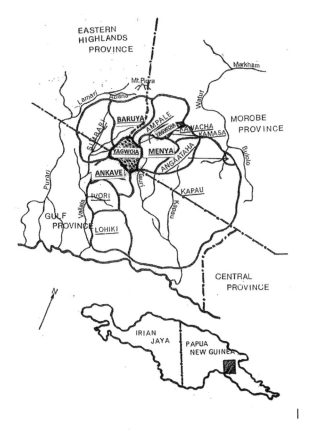

Figure 1. Map of the Angan region

Introduction

The Yagwoia-Angan people, whose selfhood I explore, live in a rugged mountainous region that stretches across the Eastern Highlands, Morobe, and Gulf provinces of Papua New Guinea (PNG). The Yagwoia population is approximately 13,000 in size, and my long-term ethnographic and linguistic fieldwork was primarily with two major groups, the Iqwaye and Iwolaqa-Malyce.[1] My concern here is to unravel from within the Yagwoia cultural imaginary their *womba* complex, a malignant condition of the soul that involves cannibalistic cravings. This condition could be easily identified as an example of "witchcraft" phenomena reported in numerous ethnographies of Melanesian lifeworlds (e.g., Stephen 1987; Reay 1976; Róheim 1948; Steadman 1975, 1985; Strathern 1982).[2]

---

1. My first ethnographic fieldwork of twenty-three months (1977–79) was followed by a stint of fifteen months between 1983 and 1986, five months in 1992, and a succession of fieldtrips ranging between one and two months in duration since then (1994–95, 1995–96, 1996–97, 1998–99, 1999–2000). In the 2000s I carried out four field trips of one month's duration each (in 2002, 2003, 2007, and 2010). Since then three of my Yagwoia coworkers have visited me in Australia (one in 2010 and two in 2017) and I am maintaining regular telephone and e-mail contact with another three who keep me informed about events in the area.

2. The present essay relates to long-term work on Yagwoia cosmology that still continues. For more detailed ethnographic

1

"Womba" as term subsumes the experience, its power, the ensuing soul-condition and transformation, and the person subject to it. I refer to all these aspects as "womba complex." The phenomena known as "witchcraft" and "sorcery" have in recent years received much coverage in international media and in anthropological debates on the PNG Highlands. However, the violence typical of reported cases of witch (and sorcerer) murder does not apply here: unlike among other groups located close-by and such elsewhere in PNG, being recognized as a womba among the Yagwoia has no lethal consequences for such a person. The critical aspect of this dynamic is that it arises from dream experience and concomitant self-recognition, not from being identified or accused by others of being a womba.

In the first four chapters, I explore the womba complex in its local cultural-existential determinations and its regional permutations in relation to shamanism. My focus is on the lived experience of the womba complex in relation to the wider context of the historical cannibalistic and mortuary practices in the Yagwoia lifeworld. I then provide an outline of how the complex relates to practices of sorcery and the mother's brother's malediction, and what these reveal about a moral sense of the self. Following a chapter that places the womba complex into a regional perspective, the study concludes with reflections on the recent escalation of witchcraft and sorcery in the PNG body social, specifically in relation to the new wave of Christian evangelism occurring in partnership with the PNG state.

Since my approach to the human condition is existential-phenomenological and psychoanalytic, my focus is on the specificities and actualities of the womba complex as an intrinsic aspect of the Yagwoia lifeworld. Thus, I seek to

---

information and a cosmo-ontological perspective on their lifeworld, see Mimica (1981, 1991); for my approach to psychoanalytic ethnography see Mimica (2003b, 2006, 2007a, 2007b, 2008b, 2009).

understand the moral fabric of the Yagwoia self-experience and intersubjectivity in its own terms, notwithstanding the clearly discernable affinities of the womba complex with the well-established anthropological category of "witchcraft." I want to avoid conceptual confusion and slippage that occurs when one employs, even as a provisional vehicle, a terminology and concepts generated through the history of external discourses that possess diverse connotations and theoretical orientations of their own making.

This tension between internal lifeworld reality and external understanding of it is further problematized by the fact that the phenomena identified as "witchcraft" and "sorcery" have, for some time now, been on the rise, namely in conjunction with the existential pressures facing PNG. These include rapid population growth, urbanization, ecological destruction, droughts and food scarcity, and the highest incidence of HIV/AIDS in the Pacific. In sum, the intensification of "witchcraft" and "sorcery" co-occur with the growing pressures of socio-economic inequalities in what was advertised in 2015 by development spin doctors as one of the fastest growing economies in the world, disregarding the fact that most of the population ekes out an existence from subsistence and cash-crop agriculture.[3]

When approached realistically, thus within the purview of the world-historical development of the capitalist world system (Braudel 1983–92; Frank 1978a, 1978b), PNG's economic situation and its mode of economic growth within the global context are better characterized as a *Raubwirtschaft* (rapine economy), whitewashed variously as "development," "modernization," "globalization," "glocalization," "cosmopolitization," or "decolonization". Correlative with this sort of dialectic of global development,

---

3. By 2016, the prospect of economic growth in PNG was characterized as "a Greek tragedy in the making" (Flanegan 2016), creating a parallel to the current financial debacle of Greece's economy.

impoverishment, pestilence, exploitation, and accumulation of wealth-and-poverty, the PNG system of state governance is consolidating into a comprador segmentary democracy whose economic basis is parasitic on natural resources, principally oil, gas, minerals, and forests. This characterization indicates the fact that at all levels of state institutions, central and regional, individuals and groups— whose primary intersubjective matrix of socialization is overwhelmingly of the segmentary tribal order—participate in schemes and transactions that cater to foreign interests and those of the national elite entangled with them, while undermining the possibility of constructive (trans) formations of local socio-economic relations and ecological conditions.

I do not share the common view that the current PNG political formation is a "failed," "dysfunctional," "fragile," or "weak state" (e.g., Dinnen 2001). This is a presumption of so many, especially of Western academics who, living in megapolitan lifeworlds, avoid contemplating a basic issue, namely that there is no intrinsic reason, let alone necessity, for such a Western political-economic institution as a "capitalist democratic state" to be universally realizable as the solely viable socio-economic framework of human existence, especially in the region known as "Melanesia." On balance, given how any state system has been functioning in the context of the last 150 years of geopolitical dynamics marked by state-mediated management of human (in) equalities, exploitation, wars, and re-construction of an intensity and magnitude unparalleled in human history,[4] the PNG comprador tribal democracy is, to use the PNG Pidgin (Tok Pisin) turn of phrase, "emi gutpela, tasol i no gutpela tu mas" (it is good although not very much good).

---

4. See, for example, Beaud (1993, 2001); Bloulet (2001); Kindleberger (1996); Landes (1998); Mann (2012, 2013); Schumpeter ([1950] 2008).

Let me outline a historically framed perspective on the Yagwoia situation within this wider context of PNG state formation and its global geopolitical entanglements. In their immediate region Yagwoia are surrounded by four other Angan peoples: Menya (to the east), Baruya and Ambale (north-northeast), Sambia (northwest), and Ankave (south-southwest) (see Map).[5] The administrative center for the Yagwoia, Menya, and Ankave regions is Menyamya on the Morobe side of the Angan region while for the Sambia and Baruya regions it is Merewaka, in the Eastern Highlands province. Four of five Yagwoia territorial groups are located in the Northwest Menyamya Census Division. For all these peoples the economic base is shifting cultivation, with the sweet potato, taro, and yam as the main cultivars, combined with cash cropping, principally coffee.

The arrival of Western civilization, that is, the capitalist world system, into this region took place in November 1950 in the form of the Australian colonial government (Hurrell 2006: 325–418).[6] Thereafter, the Yagwoia started to deal with and assimilate into their lifeworld various aspects and components of this radically exogenous human presence whose planetary-epochal self-consciousness, at that point in time, was shaped by such notions and realities as the "Nuclear Age" and the "Cold War." The Yagwoia had no idea pertaining to these radical conditions of the planetary externality; to be sure, half a century later only some of them may have some knowledge of such epochal notions. The

---

5.   The last three are well known in the anthropological literature on PNG due to the publications of Godelier (1986); Herdt (1981, 1987); and Bonnemère and Lemonnier (Bonnemère 2018; Lemonnier 2006; Bonnemère and Lemonnier 2007).

6.   There were two earlier brief encounters (in the 1930s and 1940s), but they were occluded by the one which established the Menyamya patrol post that became the tangential outpost of a radically different field of humanity, namely the world system of the capitalist civilization.

fact is that, by and large, their Western-derived education is short on Western constructions of World History and epochal self-consciousness. From the mid-1950s the way into the external regions of PNG was through recruitment into the indentured labor scheme principally catering for coastal plantations. Until the present day, going to find work and education (beyond the primary school) in outside areas remains for the majority Yagwoia, men and women, the main way out of the local lifeworld.

This colonial civilizing process went hand in hand with the introduction and use of Western technology: the first humble examples were metal tools and utensils while the latest are mobile phones. Since 2007 many, especially younger Yagwoia (aged between sixteen and forty) have become avid users of mobile phones and other digital devices, thus shaping themselves ever more into supposedly "glocal" participants in the globalized world system. However, except for cash-cropping and a meagre network of unstable vehicular roads, their region as a whole has persistently failed to realize a major breakthrough in development epitomized by a hoped-for arrival of some *kompani* (companies) that would initiate a major extractive project—be that a mining (preferably) or a logging enterprise. This is a source of intensifying frustration of living in an age of expanded horizons, fueling a bitter awareness among Yagwoia that such lucrative developments are happening elsewhere in PNG but not in their abode.

Over the years, as I have seen it happening time and again, both locally and nationally, many disadvantaged individuals rage and protest about the corruption of their elected representatives who strategically use (and abuse) government funds. But once those hitherto disgruntled get their own share, their outrage gives way to support for the reprobate politicians. Likewise with the moral outrage and promises for "an entirely new and just conduct" made by contenders for political office, ranging from village councillorship to parliamentary representation: once elected, the hitherto morally righteous contestant turns out to be of the same ilk as the one replaced.

Many world-savvy individuals are weary of and cynical about their zealous home-grown aspiring politicians and their promises, especially since as yet no mining or logging operation has been established in their territory and, accordingly, no "real" kind of development has taken place. There is nothing that many covet more than the prospect of having a mining company in their locality delivering royalties and, as it were, prosperity. The realistically mindful ones think of such infrastructural improvements as the effective maintenance of, at least, the main "all-weather" road (which would then live up to its name), well-stocked stores, and well-manned aid posts. But this sort of *kompani*-based development has not yet materialized and it is unlikely it ever will.

In the Menyamya region, Christianity was introduced in 1951 by the Australian Lutheran Mission (see Fitzpatrick 1998: 191–92). Some years later came the Seventh-Day Adventists (SDA). In the late 1960s a linguistically astute Australian Anabaptist came under the banner of the New Tribes Mission and settled in the Ambale-speaking area. Soon after he went independent and became passionately involved in the local initiation practices as well as in national politics.[7] As far as the evangelical Christian missions are concerned, their first occurrence in the Northwest Menyamya Census Division was in the mid-1980s when a White missionary family of evangelical orientation settled in the Hyaqwang-Ilyce territorial group. However,

---

7. He can be framed as an example of what I call, after Conrad ([1902] 1973), the "Kurtz complex." While serving in the national parliament he also amassed a considerable fortune that he claimed to have inherited from a deceased aunt in Australia. He died in Port Moresby, having been expelled from his "kingdom" by both his disgruntled followers and his foes who, when he lost in elections, burnt down his house.

their work did not create the kind of pneumatic stirrings commonly associated with evangelical churches that have spread all over the world, especially since the 1970s.

This changed in the new millennium with the arrival of several indigenous evangelists from what the Yagwoia called the *Rivaivelist* church. They reportedly came from the Baruya region to Hyaqwangli, in the Hyaqwang-Ilyce territorial group,[8] and originated from some other (non-Angan) region of Morobe province. What facilitated the initial attraction to and, eventually, enthusiasm for these newcomers was their successful healing of a few individuals on whom treatment by the local shamans as well as the medicine provided by medical orderlies at the Kwaplalim aid post did not work.[9] An Iwolaqa-Malyce man then invited the evangelist pastors to his area, after his wife had been successfully healed through the intervention of the Holy Spirit.[10] He became the key advocate and recruiter for the new church, and between 2003 and 2007 the pneumatic enthusiasm swept through the area, especially in one hamlet where a large number of individuals was baptized in the local Qwopali river renowned for its salt-sites. This led to a crusade of mostly young male and female converts who made their way from this area via Menyamya all the way to Kerema on the south coast and from there by ship to Port Moresby. But by 2009 this enthusiasm had subsided, and some of those dispirited admitted that, contrary to the

---

8. For the church groups in and the Christianization of the Baruya region, see Bonnemère (2016).

9. The Kwaplalim aid post was established and is supported by the Australian Lutheran Mission.

10. The man's wife had first been treated at the Kwaplalim aid post. After her recovery through the intervention of the Rivaivalists, he dismissed the work of the aid post orderlies as "rubbish" and their medicine as *pipia marasin* (Tok Pisin: rubbish medicine). They told him in response: "When you talk like that, don't come here ever again."

promises of being healed, the Holy Spirit had failed to rid them of their sicknesses. Considered in the context of the Yagwoia region as a whole, it is safe to say that only a small proportion of the population was mobilized. Presently a few small and fragmented congregations persist, confined to particular hamlets.

It should be emphasized that the Rivaivalists were met with a great deal of opposition, both from those who regard themselves as confirmed Christians (Lutheran and SDA) or from those who do not. When dealing with strangers, especially with Whites, the baseline denominational Christian self-identification for a majority of Yagwoia remains the Lutheran, irrespective of whether they are practicing Christians or not; to the best of my knowledge only a minority invokes the SDA.

My primary aim in this essay, as explained above, is to present the specificities of the Yagwoia womba complex as an intrinsic aspect of their lifeworld comprehended in terms of their cosmological self-images and institutional forms of life. Put somewhat differently, I aim to explicate the womba complex within the purview of its ouroboric cultural imaginary and, implicit in it, a distinctive cosmo-ontological matrix. "Ouroboros" is a familiar archetypal image of the serpent that eats its own tail (Jung [1967] 1976; Neumann 1970).[11] For reasons of space, I detail only the most basic lineaments of the Yagwoia cosmos.[12]

---

11. As an archetypal structure of libidinal dynamics, ouroboros crystallizes the oral-ocular-grasping (manual) unity and nucleus of all drives.

12. Given the thematic scope of this essay, I am limited as to how much ethnographic detail and argumentation I can advance in support of statements about Yagwoia cosmology, life, and specific practices, some of which will not be "self-evident." I rely on my published works (Mimica 1988, 1991, 2003a) and my PhD thesis (Mimica 1981) to provide the supporting evidential source for descriptions and interpretive statements

Correlatively, I can only hint at the way this matrix, ever since the first encounter with the Australian colonial government, has been configuring Yagwoia's assimilation of the external horizons of the capitalist world system while reciprocally, in that process, their cosmos has been slowly and steadily undergoing transfiguration into a lifeworld that, in spite of all the alterations, is sustained by and still can in various degrees and modalities reproduce its own inner existential matrix. The following will have to suffice.

As expressed in secret (esoteric) mythopoeia and various institutional forms of life, the Yagwoia cosmos is a self-created and self-generating macrocosmic androgyne whose two eyes are sun and moon. Its body is the body of the world whose navel is a place called Qwoqwoyaqwa located on a range in the Iqwaye territory. I refer to this world totality as the world-body. In the sphere of exoteric mythopoeia and common knowledge, this androgynous determination is repressed and replaced by several individuated personages, the two pivotal ones being known as Imacoqwa (Great-one-he) and his female counterpart Imacipu (Great-one-she). Thus, the suppressed bi-unity of the macrocosmic world-body is replaced by the two sexuated, separate, and individuated cosmic parents, although their matrixial inner oneness is echoed by salient affirmations of Imacoqwa's oneness, for example, "he and he alone is one who stands out, she is underneath him." One of my coworkers, deeply knowledgeable of Yagwoia mythopoeia and its derived self-images and understanding, concretely illustrated this relation by placing a longish bamboo stick into a small plastic bowl. The stick is Imacoqwa, the trunk of the cosmic tree that holds in conjunction the sky and earth; the bowl is the container, saliently the earth, although the Yagwoia image of the cosmic tree is ouroboric, that is, the branches

---

offered here. The thesis is the most complete account to date of Yagwoia cosmology, accessible by open access at the Australian National University.

and the roots intertwine. It is at once a displacement and the reprojection of the image of the cosmic androgyne whose self-closed body is locked in-on-itself by its phallus that as such is simultaneously the world-body's umbilical cord.[13]

As the two individuated cosmic parents, Imacoqwa and Imacipu are the sun and moon as well as the primordial couple from whom all humankind originated (including the White people's ancestor). It is the secret (esoteric) image of Imacoqwa as a self-created and generating androgyne that reveals its "ouroboric" determination. I use it as an apt specification of the archetypal underpinnings of Yagwoia lifeworld when comprehended as a cosmo-ontological edifice whose unique cultural expression is the cosmic androgyne in the entirety of His^Her socio-cultural manifestation.

It is important to highlight that since the introduction of Christianity the Yagwoia have been assimilating the biblical God, Jesus, the Trinity (*n/Got-tri-wan*) as well as other biblical characters (e.g., Adam, Eve, Noah, Satan) into their

---

13. Contrary to common-sense assumptions, phallus is a bisexual archetypal gestalt not reducible to the penis; rather the latter is subsumed by the former. What the above shows is one of many variants of the fundamental (un)conscious dynamic archetypal schema, namely the container^contained relation immanent in the ouroboric archetype. In this regard, the Yagwoia cosmic androgyne = world-body is also the phallic womb, that is, self-generating. It is in terms of this bisexual ouroboric gestalt that the sexuation dynamic in the Yagwoia lifeworld unfolds and the incorporative/devouring subordination of (fe)maleness can be adequately interpreted. Furthermore, its transform as the ouroboric cosmic tree (i.e., intertwining of the roots and branches) does not attenuate the erectile (upward) aspect (see Mimica 1981: 287–311; 2006: 30–36) commonly associated with the notion of the phallus. For some examples of how this phallic gestalt concretely figures in the individual (un)conscious of particular Yagwoia persons, male and female, see Mimica 2006: 38–44; 2008a).

cosmos. They became variously subsumed into and identified as Imacoqwa and other personages, for example the primal marsupial *Wuiy-Malyoqwa* (Red Man). In this regard, the most dynamic and vital dimension of this process is that of dream and visionary experiences of both ordinary individuals and such specialists in spirit(ual) affairs as shamans, or what is best glossed as "dream seers" and "spirit seers," two other categories that Yagwoia recognize. The latter can see spirits but, unlike shamans, cannot interact with and handle them; they may, however, assist shamans in healing séances. The upshot of this is that, qua the personage of Imacoqwa, there has been in the making in the Yagwoia cultural imaginary and noetic ecology[14] as a whole a particular variant of the Christian *imago Dei* that is a concrete and living presence, quite independent of the canonical ideas of the Christian God promulgated by the emissaries of whichever church and denomination. Approached in this local ouroboric perspective, the Christian God has to be grasped through diverse refractions of the autochthonous Imacoqwa, which assures the Yagwoia that although *n/Gotoqwa* (the Christian God) belongs to, as they say, "another man's book" (i.e., the White Man's Bible), He is at the same time their Imacoqwa. This sort of self-centeredness goes as far as such assertions that Jerusalem, called thus by White Man, in reality is Qwoqwoyaqwa, the local navel of the world-body.

The local cosmo-ontological determination of Yagwoia existence holds sway, in various modes and degrees, over everyone, be they educated or not, Christian or not, unyielding or indifferent toward Christianity, or embracing it but eventually giving up on making themselves into *Kristen*-s. Accordingly, the local existential flow of life^death, despite all the Christian promises of salvation, is determined by the facticity of existence rooted in the

---

14. "Noetic" is derived from the classical Greek word "nous" (mind). This is my usage for Bateson's (1973) conception of "ecology of mind."

Yagwoia world-body. To this end, the womba complex is here presented in various modalities of its experiential reality in relation to the matrixial structuration of the ouroboric flow of life^death generated from within the Yagwoia lifeworld.[15] Various ramifications of this formulation are developed in the chapters that follow.

Situated now somewhat more deeply within the Yagwoia lifeworld, let us cast another glance at the current predicament of the PNG body social. Among the over 8 million inhabitants, all the symptomatic features of "global modernity" and its so-called "glocal" variants[16] fuel for some people, such as PNG elites, varied modes of false consciousness that sustain the desires for, phantasies about, and ideologies of a good life, economic growth, and development. In parallel to them are various Christian, especially evangelical-charismatic groups that, mindful of the corruptible human nature and socio-economic inequalities, pray for the divine pneuma to infuse the body social and the nation with God's blessing and righteousness and to cleanse individual souls. But for many more the world mood is fueled by much perplexity, anxiety, frustration, chagrin, anger, and impotence, and by such universal destructive energies of the psyche as greed, jealousy, and envy.

Paralleling this currently woeful spiritual condition is a growing number of publications on the topic of witchcraft and sorcery, especially relating to the PNG Highlands. Given that these nefarious practices jar with political aspirations for economic progress and national state development held by both local elites and external stakeholders, they are mooted in various forums by anthropologists, development experts, legal professionals, government officials, and church workers. As a result, these phenomena have acquired a distinctive determination of not just being a serious

---

15. For this perspective, see especially Mimica (2003a).
16. For a critique of these usages in anthropological discourse, see Mimica (2014a).

disruption of "law and order" but something far graver: a national and international spiritual emergency subject to, at the grassroots level, practical pastoral, juridical, medical, and police intervention.[17] This "emergency" is also sounded loudly in both national and international media, largely on account of the brutally lethal consequences for many a person accused of being a witch or a sorcerer.[18]

Reading across especially the more recent anthropological and ecclesiastical literature, I see considerable confusion over, and a concomitant misconception of, indigenous realities, brought about by the use of such anthropological categories as "magic," "supernature" (Mimica 2010b), "witchcraft," and "sorcery." The latter two terms are further compounded by the varying usages of the Tok Pisin word *sanguma*, in correlation with different local phenomena that this term has historically come to subsume in different PNG lifeworlds. *Sanguma* is used to designate primarily a type of sorcery characterized as "assault sorcery" (e.g., Glick 1972), but in various parts of PNG it is also applied to "witchcraft"

---

17. I refer to only a few representative publications spanning the first fifteen years of this millennium. For the writings by Christian authors more or less directly engaged with the predicaments of people in various parts of PNG, see Bartle (2005), Gibbs (2012, 2015), Zocca (2009), and Zocca and Urame (2008). For combined anthropological, ecclesiastical, and legal cum development disquisitions, see Forsyth and Eves (2015); also Haley (2009), Jorgensen (2014), and Schram (2010).

18. The reader will find in the publications listed in the previous note numerous references to reports in PNG and Australian newspapers on witchcraft-related violence as well as to reports by Amnesty International and the United Nations. For good examples of the hype that surrounded this international outcry, see Chandler (2013) and the *Life Matters* program on ABC Radio National in June 2013. Even a glossy megapolitan magazine such as *Mindfood* (July 2018, 30–33) has an article on the "horrifying witch-hunts" in the PNG Highlands.

phenomena.[19] Mitchell (1975), citing Elkin (1964) and Warner (1958), also correctly points out the existence of an equivalent practice among Australian Aborigines. His case study of the Lujere (West Sepik) *sanguma* also clearly indicates a spectrum of permutations among the phenomena that an external categorical differentiation in terms of "witchcraft," "sorcery," "healing," "shamanism," "possession," "black/white magic," "good/evil," or "demonism" tends to screen off. Accordingly, one is likely to fail to grasp the phenomenology of reality-constitution, selfhood, morality, and value systems in relation to the dynamics and dialectics of destructive and constructive drives underpinning the overt differences between PNG lifeworlds and the ways they deal with the intersubjective realities indexed by these well-established albeit varyingly problematic anthropological categories. Furthermore, one fails to discern their relation to the fundamental structural dynamics of kinship sociality, more so since they have been distorted by the popular notions of Melanesian "dividual," "distributed," and "relational personhood" (Mimica 2010b). In order to avoid such conceptual bias, I approach the womba complex as refracted in relation to the matrixial structuration of the flow of life^death in the Yagwoia lifeworld, namely kinship and, in particular, matrifiliation. What kind of kinship personhood exists in the Yagwoia lifeworld is developed in the chapters that follow. But to understand the reality of Yagwoia personhood as a subjective reality, we have to approach these people as the kind of human beings who have no doubts that they have a soul.

---

19. For a discerning, comparative synopsis of the phenomenon and history of *sanguma*, see Mitchell (1975: 419–20, including n6); also Laycock (1996), McCallum (2006), and Franklin (2010).

CHAPTER I

The womba condition of the soul

"Soul" is a gloss for the vernacular *umpne*, the primary meanings of which are the warmth of breath and the accompanying hissing sound of breathing (exhalation). It foregrounds a sensory quality of the animating heat that permeates and sustains bodily vitality. An alternative word is *umdinye* (or *umdne*), which specifies more focally the thermal (heat) modality, while *umpne* emphasizes the sonic-breathing modality. Accordingly, "soul" should be understood in the first instance as the vital thermal-breath animating energy, in the sense of a generative motility-activity, immanent in the body. Since it is conterminous with the bodily substantiality,[1] one always has to think of various modalities and transformations of this life energy in relation to its (dis)embodiment and transformations correlative with the synergy between human embodiment (microcosmos) and the world-body (macrocosmos). As a first approximation, the dynamic relation between the world-body and all its denizens is that of the ouroboric container that generates, from within itself, all its contents.

---

1. The category "substance" is not taken for granted (see Mimica n.d.). However, precisely because it is embodied in and determined by the qualities of bodily quiddity, the Yagwoia soul, its quiddity, can also be characterized as a substance, hence spoken of as soul-substance.

The basal animating heat-breath modality of the soul is distinguished as the *aama umpne* (person-soul) whose inception is in the heat and the paternal implantation of semen into the maternal womb during sexual intercourse. When a person dies, this animating heat has ceased, and the body undergoes metamorphosis manifest as germination, spectacular bloating, liquefaction, and decomposition of the flesh, a mirror-reversal of the gestation process, while the soul (that is, animating heat-breath) transforms into a *wopa ilymane* (spirit of the dead).[2] In the course of an infant's growth, its *umpne* is subject to development whereby it becomes differentiated into several semi or fully detachable or, more accurately, ex-corporative-incorporative components. These are also lexically distinguished.

Accordingly, the *umpne* constellation has to be comprehended as forming a dynamic field of functionally differentiated and varyingly individuated and volatile potencies (components), at once unitary and plural. It is embodied yet subject to disembodiment as well as to a temporary and/or permanent loss of some of its components. The last condition pertains to various potencies (including shamanistic ones), which can be acquired as a boon from the wild forest spirits that, as acquisition, can also be lost again. These potencies are thought and often spoken of as being autonomous agencies and as such forming a number of individual and different souls. What is critically important to grasp is that the Yagwoia soul-constellation constitutes

---

2. *Wopa ilymane* literally means "sweet potato spirit." The characterization indicates that the spirits of the dead hang around homesteads, feeding as it were on the leftovers of the living humans' staple food—sweet potato. Folk etymology derives the word from *ilyce-mane* (feces road/passage, that is, anus) since, first, the corpse decomposition is conterminous with extreme stench and, second, the deceased spirit is shown the anus during the mortuary rites (see Mimica 2006) and thus repelled from the abode of the living.

a realm of experience and action that can be rendered as their "subjectivity," except that it is not something delimited by the body as an exclusive "interiority" vis-à-vis the "exteriority" of the world. Nor does one's *umpne* coincide with one's egoity or I-ness. Rather, the latter is subject to the field of its *umpne*, which pertains simultaneously to both the threshold of bodily interiority and the exteriority of the world-body. The *umpne* constellation itself is opened and/or closed to the influences of and afflictions by the various denizens and powers that exist in the world-body.

At the core of the *umpne* constellation is *kune umpne*, best glossed as "thought/thinking soul" or "noetic soul"; its manifestation becomes especially evident in infants at the onset of speaking activity. It is one's soul that does the thinking/speaking and that is the agency driving one's actions and volition (see further below). Another differentiated component, usually spoken of in a generic sense as *ngalye umpne* (my soul),[3] detaches from a sleeping person's body and goes off wandering—and thus generating dreams; they are external experiences that take place in the external existential dimension of the world-body. Another aspect of the human soul is its manifestation in various animal appearances, for example, a bee, mouse, mantis, lizard, or cockroach. As such it may be physically harmed, beaten for instance, which in turn will show up as a bruise or wound on the affected person's body. A person may die from such an assault. Furthermore, shamans or curers[4] acquire,

---

3. Individuals differ in their views as to whether this dream-soul component is one's *kune umpne* (some insist that it never leaves the body in which it is "like a stone," that is, immovable in respect of the body) or a separate soul-agency, for which different speakers may offer several labels.

4. In Yagwoia shamans or curers are *aa'mnye nabalye iye*, literally "person sickness do-beater," that is, extractors of sickness. In the Yagwoia lifeworld most sicknesses are various objects that get lodged directly into the body or indirectly affect it by being

as a boon from the wild spirits, multiple potencies that are spoken of as their multiple souls or individualized agencies.

The Yagwoia embodiment is, however, a microcosmic instantiation of the world-body. In this determination *umpne* (in its form of animating heat) is generated by the motion of blood through the "blood ropes" and the bone marrow within the skeleton pivoting on its spinal axis. Both blood and marrow are replenished through eating. These two vital circuits are the equivalents of the differential macrocosmic circuits of the sun and moon whose intertwined thermal-liquid-luminous qualities generate and sustain, together with the fluvial and pluvial flows, the animation and life of the world-body as a whole. The macrocosmic embodiment (container) is the ouroboric androgyne Imacoqwa who embodies (contains) and generates Him^Herself and, in the process, everything that exists, including the human microcosmos (Mimica 1981, 1988, 1991). The sun and moon are his two eyes. There is a ceaseless synergy between the macrocosmos and the microcosmos, mediated by the wild forest spirits (*hyaqaye ilymane*) and, post-mortem, the spirits of the dead (*wopa ilymane*).

The wild spirits are ambisexual and cannibalistic,[5] and cause various afflictions, some of which are the source of

---

placed in particular locations of the world-body by spirits and/or human beings. The Tok Pisin labels "*glasman/meri*" capture some characteristics of Yagwoia curers. However, the translation of these terms in some recent literature as "diviner" is misleading. By contrast, and regardless of the amount of ink that has been spilled on the problematic of shamanism, the mode of being and craft of Yagwoia curers is served well by the label "shamans."

5.   Since the wild spirits are spirits (that is, seemingly nonhuman), it may be objected that they cannot therefore be "cannibalistic." However, once understood in the perspective of the Yagwoia cosmo-ontological framework of intelligibility, specifically the implications of the macrocosmic > < microcosmic constitution of selfhood and the "person," the "human/

shamanistic power and endowments of the living human soul; in fact, one can only become a shaman by becoming affected and thereby (s)elected by the wild spirits. The spirits of the dead, specifically those of the maternal relatives (all classed as "mothers"),[6] account for most sicknesses that befall the Yagwoia. The paternal spirits of the dead, by contrast, are invariably protective of their living issue (progeny). I highlight here the fundamental fact of the ambivalence of the spirit powers inherent in the world-body. They are capable of both benevolence and malignancy.[7] In this kind of cosmos, "generation" is a totalizing life^death process where living and dying are the at once polarized and semi-differentiated modalities of the ceaseless auto-generative flow of the world-body (Mimica 1996, 2003a).[8]

---

nonhuman" differentiation acquires a distinctively Yagwoian determination. For a cosmo-ontological elucidation of what the wild forest spirits are, see Mimica (2003a).

6. The Yagwoia kinship system is an extreme Omaha type: not only are the MZ and all females whom my mother calls "sister" my "mothers," but also my MB, MBS, MBD, MBSS, MBSD, and so forth, that is, all direct "bone" descendants of my "base MB" (3S *qaule kayemu*). What has to be highlighted then is that one has both female and male "mothers." The term for the base MB (thus the MB who is of the same birth order as my mother), 1S *namnoqwa*, literally means "my mother's breast."

7. For a cosmo-ontological interpretation of the difference between the wild forest spirits and the spirits of the dead, see Mimica (2003a).

8. There is no such a cosmic-existential realm as "supernature and supernatural" agencies in the Yagwoia lifeworld (see Mimica 1981, 2010b). Accordingly, although most sicknesses and so many ensuing deaths are caused by the spirits of deceased *maternal* relatives (male and female mothers), this fact does not make these deaths "unnatural" or seen as brought about by "nonnatural" or "supernatural" causes. If a person dies due to sorcery, then that is the cause of death,

The nose-piercing act (first male initiation), which until the late 1950s also included induction into the long-term practice of fellatio, is the one that "ruptures" the novices' maternal (flesh) *umpne* and ignites the germinating flow of the bone-marrow = seminal *umpne* (heat), equivalent to the solar heat of the macrocosmic body.[9] The maternal blood heat, equivalent to the lunar cool liquidity, thereby becomes attenuated and balanced down so that the novices' bodies become progressively hardened, that is, bone-like and thus solarized. The ritual *inekiye* house with its internal cosmic tree edifice (Mimica 1981) was the living semblance and the mediating ritual conduit of the ceaseless synergetic inter-flow of life^death between the macrocosmic world-body and the human microcosmic bodies. The *inekiye* presents an exoteric image of the world-body. The cosmic-tree edifice with intertwined branches and roots is its skeleton (equivalent to the skeleton, the bone marrow, and the semen in the microcosmic human body). In the context of the first initiation ceremony this ouroboric arboreal edifice is ritually activated so that it becomes the conduit for the luno-solar heat-effluence of the macrocosmic body.[10] The

---

indeed, a variant of homicide, but sorcery no less than spirits are not "unnatural" or "supernatural" agents/causes. In fact, spirits are just as "natural" denizens of the Yagwoia lifeworld as humans, souls, pigs, dogs, or worms. In Mimica (1996) and further developed in Mimica (2010b), I discuss a whole range of existential meanings of different occurrences of death, showing in the process that the common anthropological notion of "(un)natural" deaths is simply out of place in a lifeworld such as the Yagwoia.

9. For details concerning Yagwoia initiations, see Mimica (1991: 95–109); for the regulation of homosexual relations (semen-givers/receivers), see Mimica (1991: 105–109).

10. It is in reference to this total ritual and cosmological complex of the life-flow "energetics" of the world-body in relation to the human microcosmic embodiment and its development that I can thematize the problematic of such a concept as

tree-edifice in turn attracts wild forest spirits who afflict individual novices, thus endowing them with shamanistic powers. However, these afflictions are not specific to the first initiation and any person, male or female, may be seized at any time by a wild spirit, usually in the forest.

With the irrevocable cessation of male initiation in early 2000, this ritual mediation and control of the vital, even energetic, dynamics of Yagwoia bodily existence was effectively terminated.[11] The Yagwoia men who underwent initiation at a time when fellatio was still in practice were of the opinion, in some respects quite accurately, that the cessation of insemination had led to the shortening of the duration of bachelorhood, that is, an exclusive homosexual life tied to the bachelors' house. This in turn led to a much earlier commencement of men's heterosexual career (thus marriage) and, concomitantly, stimulated the decline of their sexual self-restraint, leading to an increase in the frequency of pregnancy among women and a decrease in the spacing of children. In consequence, children do not spend enough time on the mother's breast, so that their bodies are not as strong as those of previous Yagwoia

---

"spirit," considered as a potency-aspect of their souls. In their Tok Pisin usage the soul is called "spirit" (derived from English) but it would be misleading to accept it uncritically. On the other hand, the luno-solar determination of *umpne/ umdinye* and the psychosexual foundations of their lifeworld and its historical vicissitudes amplify the essential psycho-sexual quiddity of the Yagwoia soul-constellation and, as such, facilitates its interpretation within the framework of psychoanalytic and Jungian conceptualization of libido as "psychic energy," projected onto the world at large.

11. On the historical vicissitudes of Yagwoia initiation practices, see Mimica (1991: 94–98). The irrevocable cessation started already in the second half of the 1980s when what was to be the last cycle of initiations, which had commenced in 1983, was unfolding with differential durations and perseverance among the four central Yagwoia territorial groups.

generations.[12] This decline in the domain of the bodily microcosmos was especially emphasized in reference to the generations of men who, following the abandonment of homosexuality, became subject to a double deprivation: not only did boys not spend enough time on the mother's breast due to more frequent pregnancies but, in the absence of fellatio, their initiation experience became void of the primordial (cosmogonic) seminal nourishment that would make their bodies imbued with the kind of bone strength that the generations of the men of yore used to embody. With the terminal end of the initiations this vital decline of the Yagwoia body social has intensified and the view of both senior men and women, also acknowledged by so many younger individuals, is that the present generations are all weaklings and no match for their predecessors. Even so, their macro^micro cosmic container^contained determination of existence continues in all vigor: it is articulated through kinship within which human bodily beings are generated (copulation > gestation > birth > feeding and care) as are sicknesses and deaths (dissolution and re-incorporation into the world-body).

What has to be emphasized is that, in the context of their traditional lifeworld, the Yagwoia existential process was never subject to a salvational project or, in a more general characterization within the horizon of world history, they never came under the spell of the "transcendental break-through" that characterizes "axial civilizations" (Jaspers 1953; also Eisenstadt 1986; Bellah and Joas 2012). Their "spirituality"—interaction with sundry souls, spirits, and denizens inhabiting their lifeworld—is neither celestial nor chthonic but, as the image of their ouroboric cosmic tree clearly shows, the two poles are intertwined. In a nutshell: in this lifeworld there never was (and still is not) salvation nor damnation, ergo no "heaven" and "hell," only the ceaseless process of life^death. It is symptomatic how this aspect

12. For the Yagwoia view of breastfeeding and weaning, see ch. 2.

of Yagwoia existence impacted on the first evangelical missionary, a young American who came to work in one of the Yagwoia territorial groups in the mid-1980s. I encountered him only once. When I remarked to him that the Australian Lutheran Mission had been Christianizing Yagwoia since the early 1950s and asked whether he would not, therefore, think that they were sufficiently Christian, he replied: "No, we don't think that these people are Christians; they don't believe in heaven and hell, good and evil!" Even with the acceptance of Christianity by some Yagwoia, the salvation of their souls is very much in question as are all the promises of the God from the Bible, which some of them pointedly call "another man's book," not to mention the total absence of the Socratic-Platonic conception of the soul and ethical life that shaped Christian (as well as Jewish and Islamic) notions of the soul, self, person, ethics, and the (trans)formation of the superego (conscience) in relation to the almighty God (e.g., Elkasisy-Friemuth and Dillon 2009; Adluri 2013).

One must be mindful of the fact that the reality of the Yagwoia lifeworld, irrespective of how "glocalized" it may be, is nevertheless generated and sustained from within and by its noetic ecology, thus one that is, as they say of themselves and their language and customs, of "this earth" (world-body), with the post (*hilace*, *angice*; axis mundi) that holds the earth in conjunction with the sky located in Qwoqwoyaqwa, their navel (the cosmic center). Clearly a product of the human archetypal imagination, these cosmic self-images and their concrete local actualizations are, nevertheless, a singular Yagwoia formation that has its roots in the primary Papuan stratum of New Guinea ecologies of mind that implanted their roots in this region of the planet some 60,000 years ago and flourished ever since, very much on their own terms. Accordingly, by accepting the singular reality of this regional spatio-temporal vortex one also acknowledges that such categories as "body," "sex/gender difference," "person," "morality," "good" and "bad," and "sky^earth" (the world-as-a-whole) have different existential valencies and meanings precisely because their lifeworld, as any other in Melanesia, is a singular universal individuated in the field of physical and noetic ecologies that historically had limited involvements with the Euro-Asian civilizational fields and their axial cosmological projects and pursuits (e.g., Seaford 2016; Obeyesekere 2002, 2012). This also extends to their appropriation of the Christian God and ways that commenced in 1952. Correlatively, terms such as "soul," "body," and "spirit" are used here as shorthand English glosses that must be thought with in terms of the cosmo-ontological meanings of the Yagwoia ouroboric world-body (macrocosmos) and the cosmology as a whole.[13]

The causes and attributes of womba soul affliction and shamanistic treatment

A person becomes a womba because his/her soul has been afflicted by the soul of someone who him/herself is a womba or by a spirit. The former is by far the most common cause of this kind of affliction. Everyone can succumb to it and, indeed, many Yagwoia persons have had the experiences that induce the womba affliction; this may become a persistent predicament albeit one that manifests only sporadically. The diagnostic experience is recurrent dream visions in which the focal scenario is of the dreamer being tempted to eat either pig-meat (raw, cooked, and/or putrid) and/or human flesh.[14] Desiring or eating raw pig-meat in dreams

---

13. These meanings, in turn, require further explication in reference to the overall ouroboric structure and dynamics of Yagwoia cosmology. For more details concerning this summary, see Mimica (1981; 1991; especially 2003a: 262–65, 274–77).

14. In this respect a vital conditioning dimension of the Yagwoia womba complex is their mortuary practices. These involve prolonged exposure to a decomposing corpse and formerly

is commonly the precursor for eating human flesh, which can also be either raw and/or putrid. Usually, one cannot discern the agent who offers the meat, but it is taken for granted that it is a womba (i.e., his/her soul). It can also be spirits (*ilymane*) since these are a permanent presence in the Yagwoia reality and, whenever a person falls asleep, his/her soul enters into that existential dimension. The vital preventive step against becoming a full womba is to tell other people about the dream-showing. The dream visions may continue, and in many cases they do, but their power has already been diffused by virtue of the fact that they are publicly known. If one keeps silent, one will see more and more of this kind of showings (*ucoqwalye*) and, by holding these inside, one's soul (*umpne*) will become habituated and turn one into a womba. That is, the soul comes to crave raw pig and/or human flesh and will no longer want to give it up. I emphasize here that it is a nexus of appetite and desire for porcine meat = human flesh that thus becomes a permanent fixture and craving of one's soul. The afflicted person is advised to seek a shaman who will literally remove the womba imprint from the soul, and this will at least temper and defuse, if not eradicate, the condition. However, the consensus is that it is the person himself/herself who must desire to be rid of it, otherwise the shaman's exorcism may have only an interminable effect. For example, after a treatment the person may stop having such dream-showings for quite a long time, but then they may start to occur again. Another shamanic treatment will be sought with the same result, and so it can carry on indefinitely (see ch. 3). What should be highlighted is that becoming/being

---

also included a form of mortuary endo-cannibalism focused on the ingestion of bodily fluids (see Mimica 1991, 2003a, 2006, 2008c). A detailed psycho-dynamic elucidation of this complex unravels its intrinsic necrophiliac and necrophagous aspects in relation to its roots in the ouroboric matrix of the Yagwoia (un)conscious (see ch. 4).

a womba is not a matter of "somebody accusing me of being one" (as for instance in "witchcraft accusations") but, rather, it is I who, through my dream experience, recognizes this affliction without the mediation of others: it is a matter of self-recognition.

Nonetheless, the condition is not one of total soul-entrapment. Shamans can potentially remove the womba imprint from a person's soul. The treatment technique is the same as for other sicknesses. Yagwoia shamans, male and female, depend on acquired soul potencies: these are agencies with particular healing powers and the power of penetrating vision. These potencies are thought and spoken of as individual souls and as such can be also glossed as soul-familiars. All of these are a boon from the wild forest spirits, with the acquisition of the vision power further involving the agency of the sun (see Mimica n.d.). This primary power is metonymically expressed in the Tok Pisin nomination *glasman* (glass + man) or *glasmeri* (glass + woman). "Glass" indicates the power of the curer's vision that penetrates the body like a torch-beam (an informant's description), that is, renders it transparent, like through a glass, so that the sickness object lodged inside the body becomes visible. The vernacular name for shaman is *aa'mnye nabalye iye* (literally, person sickness-object doer). It indexes the most obvious aspect of the shaman's craft, the extraction of malignant objects and/or spirits responsible for sickness. This pivotal activity is literally the beating out (*napalye pice-qale*) of a sickness object. In the initial curing procedure the shaman also sprinkles water and beats and rubs (cleans) the afflicted body part with a bundle composed of *waquye* (indigenous begonia), one or two (commonly red) *wogaye* (cordyline) leaves, and one or two other plants with a distinctive smell. All but *waquye* are optional. *Waquye*, like all plants in the Yagwoia lifeworld, is of female quiddity whereas *wogaye*, being more like a tree, is male; they figure in Yagwoia social classification as female and male endearment names (*ilaye yeuwye*). Thus, the shamanistic bundle is a conjunction of the male^female generative plant substance that together with water is applied to the body subjected to the penetrating-extractive manipulation. A third penetrating element is the shaman's breath that, in the mode of directed whistle-blowing, combines both the oral-sonic and the heat-pressure qualities coming from inside of his/her body and as such is iconic of the generic quiddity of the soul (*umpne* = heat-breath).[15]

What has to be emphasized in this composition of the shamanistic plant bundle is its libidinal auto-generative determination. In the Yagwoia lifeworld, no substance is inert. Any mode of substance is generative of either malignant or benign qualities and effects. For instance, any sickness object is itself a negative generative substance (in a sexual-metabolic sense) that actively generates its destructive power, clearly manifest in the very condition of the afflicted body and its correlative sensory experience, such as pain, high temperature, loss of flesh, and weakness. In a fundamental sense, the sickness process itself can be characterized as the eating of the body by the sickness-object or some other kind of agent responsible for the affliction. The shaman's bundle, a composite of male^female plant matter, is a living (organic) self-generating unit and precisely as such is an effective instrument of the shaman's extractive craft. Moreover, it can be characterized as the manual isomorph of the shaman's phallic (penetrating) vision.

The shaman concurrently blow-whistles over the targeted body spot and beats over it until the sickness pops

---

15. As an energic entity, the soul is also made present through the plants' scent, which is a cross-modal sensory equivalent of heat and breath. Furthermore, the name of one plant (*ampne* or *amdne*) contains the morphemic components of the words for soul (*umpne* or *umdinye*), amplifying the sensory-iconic unity of plant bundle, breath-whistle, and bodily quiddity of the soul.

or shoots out. Exactly the same is done when a malignant spirit (most commonly of a deceased maternal relative) is whipped from the body into a receptacle made from a banana leaf, rolled for this purpose into a funnel. When the spirit is beaten into the funnel, the curer gives it a violent blow with both hands, squashes and twists it as hard as possible, and throws it into the fire. Thus, the diacritical ocular-manual penetrative > beating > extractive action is a mode of exorcism.[16] During the early stages of affliction, the shaman may also create a protective space around the sufferer's body by encircling it with a burning piece of tapa dyed with the juice of the red pandanus (*hyamauce*).[17] The shaman may also delegate one of his spirit-familiars to watch over the sufferer and prevent the latter from being re-invaded by the malignant spirit. These same protective and

---

16. Moreover, objects such as cowrie shells (indigenous currency) are also subject to exorcising action when they become possessed by the spirits of their deceased owners. As they were possessive of their valuables in life, these spirit owners become permanently lodged in the shells after death. A new owner of these objects comes to suspect that they may be *ilyma-ungye* (spirit shells) when falling sick after acquiring these objects. Shamans are called upon to diagnose if this is the case since no other villager will want to accept these objects in transactions. Many a shell-exorcism is unsuccessful so that the only solution is to get rid of the shells through exchange with individuals from other, basically non-Yagwoia speaking groups (e.g., Baruya, Ankave); that is, to let foreigners suffer the possessiveness of the local deceased owners. In general, Yagwoia have realistic expectations regarding the efficiency of their shamans. Every shamanistic treatment is subject to vicissitudes: the outcome can be wholly positive but in the main is only a temporary success, and there is no shortage of failures. One goes on living and suffering from one treatment to the next.

17. One does not have to be a shaman to execute this protective action (see the case of OMitane in ch. 3).

capturing techniques apply to the exorcism of the womba-afflicted soul. However, it is the person's soul that has to be divested of the affliction rather than that there literally is an object or a possessing spirit lodged in it. This is why the shaman's action is vitally dependent on the sufferer's own will or, better, the sufferer's engagement with the own soul (see ch. 3). Only in this way can the afflicted expel the womba imprint produced by the recurrent womba showings.

A fully developed womba soul is cannibalistic through and through. The typical modus operandi is that the womba soul penetrates the victim's body, drinks blood, eats vital organs (*qalye*), especially the liver, and replaces them with a banana leaf or a piece of bark. After such an attack, the person bleeds internally, quickly deteriorates, and dies. No shaman can help the victim. However, if only a portion of the liver has been eaten, the shaman can treat it by taking half a pig or bird liver and attaching this, together with a cassowary feather, to the damaged liver, which will eventually heal. To be exact, it is the shaman's soul component, which has the specific potency (acquired from the forest spirits) for this kind of cure, that effects the healing. The womba-person also eats live pigs or, reportedly though less commonly, marsupials, that is, game animals. The pig's owner can identify such an occurrence when an animal suddenly becomes skinny, despite having been fed regularly. Furthermore, a womba-person can assume an animal appearance, most commonly of a pig, and roam about the place damaging gardens (see ch. 2). In terms of appearance, a womba-person is skinny with opossum-like red eyes and blood-dripping hands.

The womba-person is aware of his/her soul's propensity and activity. Moreover, such a soul can attack other persons regardless of whether they are asleep or wakeful. A person may be engaged in friendly conversation while being cannibalized by the womba soul. However, not everyone is equally exposed to such attacks. If a potential victim is asleep and thus more vulnerable but has a strong *umpne*, this will fight off the attacker. Yet a person whose soul is not strong will be easy prey. In general, therefore, sick and physically enfeebled persons are more vulnerable. Given that the *umpne* with womba propensity will act regardless of whether the person qua his/her volitional I-ness may wish so, those involved in the butchering at pig kills may mutter spells to parry such an eventuality. On one such occasion Qang, one of my coworkers, commented sotto voce that there may always be someone present whose womba soul is attracted by the spectacle of butchering and the carved pig-meat.

These characteristics of the womba-person reflect a commonly upheld stereotypical image that is readily verbalized when one inquires about this soul condition. Interlocutors are also likely to say in this context that womba-persons were more common in the past than they are nowadays. The image has salience as an explicit figure within the intersubjective imaginary of the Yagwoia lifeworld. Yet, as we shall see, this image is at variance with the actual figurations of concrete experiences of womba showings and concomitant predicaments suffered by so many individuals: for in this visionary oneiric dimension, the semblance of the actual womba, instrumental in these showings, seems never to be revealed. Nevertheless, these two dimensions of the complex complement and sustain each other.

The case of Qang

The way in which my coworker Qang accounted his own life highlights all the main diagnostic features of womba dream visions. This is what he told me. Qang would have been in his mid to late twenties, married with children, when he underwent the tribulations of a womba experience. He had recurrent dream visions. The typical oneiric scenario was a place where a pig is killed and dispatched. Its vital organs, entrails, red meat, and fat were placed on a tree branch, with the blood dripping down. The man who was dispatching the pig did not talk to Qang (the dreamer) or the people in his company, namely Qang's sister and her husband (that is, the dreamer's ZH, an affine [*kamba*]). To be sure, persons figuring in dreams are semblances whose identity is not taken at face value; they are primarily taken as spirits and/ or souls who can assume the semblance of known persons, living or dead. The man who bore semblance of the dreamer's ZH told him to taste some of the raw meat. To demonstrate, he took a red cordyline leaf that was dripping with blood and ingested it. Then he told the dreamer: "You try it! It tastes good" (*ilayi'na'nyi iqu'natana*). The dreamer followed his example and "thus now, it was good and palatable." The woman who looked like his sister then brought him the pig's head and he broke it lengthwise down the middle. This time he was the first one to taste, after which he gave one half of the head to his sister. Still dreaming, he tried a piece of cooked (*pace*) pork but found that it was not tasty and that he did not like it, but when he tried a piece of raw (*yena*) meat, he did like it. The fact that he partook of the raw meat and its effect—namely his subsequent *dislike* of cooked meat—was the decisive experience that proved to him that he had succumbed to a womba.

Dream after dream Qang experienced the same events. Although disturbed by these malignant showings, he knew how to deal with them. He summoned his wife and children and told them that "if you feel that a womba has been eating you, then you look no further; it is not some other person but me who does it to you. Because I've been dreaming this all the time and it has shown me (*ucoqwalye*, that is, taught my soul) this." In reference to the fact that he was endowed with cannibalistic potency instead of his soul being shown visions, ordinarily induced by a wild forest spirit and that would have given it shamanistic powers, he explained: "And this—I am not a dog or a wild forest spirit, so that I'll turn back on eating man."

What has to be highlighted here is that Qang did not actually eat human flesh. Yet, his self-understanding, the advice he gave his family, and the way he evaluated the dream explicitly affirm the transitivity of the intra-oneiric experience of eating raw pig-meat and pig-blood in relation to human flesh: the former inevitably effects the latter.[18] The reason for this is not just their fundamental identity. Rather, as I shall detail later, in the Yagwoia lifeworld all consumable substances, especially meat but also other kinds of things, derive their substantial quiddity and identity from the substantiality of the human body. The way in which Qang expressed the cannibalistic desire (as "turning back" from the seemingly nonhuman = raw pig-meat to the human flesh) renders him akin to a dog and the cannibalistic wild forest spirits, although the latter are also the source of soul potencies, such as certain forms of shamanistic healing power. The "turning back" specifically implies the Yagwoia view of incest as self-copulation, and its correlate of self-eating, which is what the invocation of the dog pictures, namely the male canine practice of licking its own penis (Mimica 1991) and the view that pigs and dogs do not discriminate as to who copulates with whom: parents with their own offspring, siblings with each other. They know nothing of the kind of order that is human kinship relatedness.

However, since Qang quickly revealed his visions, they ceased and with them his worries. What should be stressed here in the first place is his concern with the wellbeing of his wives and children whom he saw as the most likely target of his afflicted soul. This alone gives weight to his self-evaluation as a "good person" compromised by the unwanted malignant influence of some womba whose

---

18. See Reay (1962) for a similar identification of pig-meat = human meat in dreams among the Kuma of the Central Highlands. The Kuma did not practice cannibalism and regarded it abhorrent, but they attributed it to witches.

identity was fundamentally indeterminate—despite the fact that the crucial person in the dream scenario was his ZH. In no way did Qang think that his ZH was the womba and was responsible for his affliction. In fact, if any one of the persons manifest in the dream could be suspected of being the culprit, then it would be the anonymous man who killed the pig. Be that as it may, what matters is that the dreamer held himself culpable for any malignant effects that might ensue from the new condition of his soul. As for how he might be seen by his fellow villagers, Qang said: "They'll say, 'There comes a womba-man,' and I'll feel shame. But I am a good man, yet my soul knows to eat man! So why should I be ashamed?!"

Here we see clearly indicated the horizon of I-ness in Yagwoia experience. One is literally the subject of one's own soul and all sorts of experiences and conditions that it may suffer/endure but that, as such, do not translate into the agentive volitional activities of one's own I-ness. For the Yagwoia, the irreducible locus of one's "I" (or ego) is specifically one's own bodily flesh; it belongs to one's own mother and, through her, to all the other mothers. The critical ones, as mentioned earlier, are one's true male mothers—MB, MBS, MBD, MBSS, and MBSD—that is, the direct "bone" descendants of one's "base MB" (*qaule kayemu*). The point is that the agentive-volitional scope and actions of one's soul, its desires as well as passions, do not coincide with the locus and the scope of one's egoity; and yet, willy-nilly, the latter is subjected to the former and one always has to come to terms with what one's soul may foist (for good or bad) upon one in relation to all sorts of other agents external to it. So, in Qang's case, his soul became infused with a cannibalistic desire but, and this is essential, he did not give in to the malignancy that had befallen him. And by "talking out"—note that this was not some public confession but an announcement to his wives and children in order to protect them from his own cannibalistic malignancy—he prevented its full realization. Moreover, there was no need for any shamanistic intervention to eradicate the malignancy of his soul since his "talking out" had fully worked.

The desire for pig-meat

Given the centrality of the desire for pig-meat and, in general, meat/flesh in the womba complex, a comment will serve as the thematically relevant background for the chapters that follow. Although there are certain differences in diet for men and women, these do not warrant a discussion in relation to the womba complex.[19] The fact is that, with the exception of some individuals (male and female) who are not particularly keen on pork, both men and women do desire pork and game meat.[20] A Yagwoia woman will readily

---

19. The same holds true for the factuality of hunger. There have always been fluctuations in the local climatic conditions and in the actual availability of food, the most important being the sweet potato. Thus, actual hunger is a contingent component of the Yagwoia food ecology, and it would be naive to foreground it as a factor that significantly conditions the womba complex.

20. One person who has to forego eating pork (and chewing betel nuts) for the rest of his life is the male custodian of the *Wiye latice* (discussed in greater details in ch. 3) prior to assuming the role of nose-piercer (and other functions belonging to this position). The son he chooses to succeed him in this role has to do the same. When the Yagwoia first learned that the same sort of taboo is a pre-requisite for admission into the SDA church, some joked that its ancestor must have been the *Wiye* ancestor. It is precisely because of the prohibition of pork and betel nuts that the majority of Yagwoia are not attracted to the SDA version of Christianity. The food taboos applied to first-stage initiates include, among others, the prohibition of pork, betel-nut chewing, and the juice of red pandanus.

chastise her man (husband)[21] for failing to provide her with pork and/or game (marsupial), which is a basic way for him to show his care for her. This extends to such items as tinned fish, meat, and rice. There is always a libidinal undertone to this provisioning and its failure. Confronted with this sort of rebuke, men will readily feel impotent, especially if the reference is to game (marsupials), for this targets his abilities as a hunter.

A common preamble to coaxing a woman into (especially extramarital) sex is to offer her a fine piece of pork. This practice is known as the *yaqaalye lakice* (literally pig-penis), a term that can be glossed as "pork-for-sex." One can indeed say that a piece of pork will surely get you a long way into Yagwoia hearts—male and female.[22] There are also acute domestic situations that can provoke gossip among villagers. The following is typical: a man has attended a pig

---

21. The Yagwoia terms for spouses do not correspond to "wife" and "husband." They use "woman" and "man," as in "my woman" (*ngalye aapale*) or "my man" (*ngalye qwole*). This is the terminology I generally use in the text, though I might resort to "husband" and "wife" if necessary for clarity.

22. Both men and women pursue extramarital sex, this being the principal cause of cross-sex accusations, recriminations, abuse of women, and deadly fights between men, especially those who are related as "brothers," both agnatic and classificatory matrilateral. It is symptomatic that in the context of the first initiations when the novices are given (inculcated) the "word of counsel," effectively the Yagwoia code of male moral behavior, one of the precepts they are told is that one should "not copulate with your co-initiates' and your brothers' women." Most intra-group homicide cases are due to extramarital relations, and many of these are fratricides. "Promiscuous" and "lascivious" aspects of Yagwoia sexuality are both men's and women's attributes and when it comes to active sex seeking, men and women have equipollent desires, notwithstanding men's projections that they are the victims of women's insatiable desire.

kill where he ate some pork without sparing a bit for his wife or wives. It is held that eating pork produces a glossy shine on the face, and especially around the mouth, of the eater. By and large, this is true. This irradiation, on par with the porcine odor of breath, lasts for quite a while so that one cannot simply wipe it off. It is difficult to conceal the cause of such a symptomatic radiance of the face, so that the man's woman (or women) will quickly suspect him and accuse him of shameful stinginess.[23]

It can be said of both men and women that their desire for pork (and meat in general) is equipollent and has no bounds; as such it may give rise to various manipulations of its object in order to consummate it. I once forgot all about a sizeable piece of pork, cut from a bigger chunk, that I had purchased for some of my friends. The piece began to stink, and I was about to throw it away when two men who were visiting me begged me not to waste what they saw as a still salvageable and therefore "good = edible" piece of pork. They would boil it for a long time, which would make it good enough to eat, they said. I protested, fearing that they might get food poisoning, but to no avail. They assured this was a safe procedure. After boiling the meat for a good hour, they ate the piece with utmost relish, to the amusement of a few onlookers, amplified by the fact that everyone else were not keen on partaking of it and the two did not have to share. While gulping down the pieces, they joked that they were womba on the account of eating pork that stank.

---

23. Some such cases gain notoriety when the culprit winds up with a bad stomach and has to vomit; his woman (or women), who all along knows the cause of his predicament, will not hesitate to inspect the evacuated contents for the incriminating evidence, which is sure to intensify her rebuke and, correlatively, his hapless entrapment.

CHAPTER 2

Men and women as womba

Over the many years of my research among the Iqwaye-Yagwoia, I have personally known only two men whose souls were irremediably fixated by the womba affliction and everybody knew it. They are presented in this chapter as Qwoqwoldate and WoGaye. Most of what I have to say about them I learned from their fellow villagers of different ages. In that respect, the following accounts for the way these two men figure in the intersubjective realm of their lifeworld and sociality, that is, as they are seen and engaged with by their fellow villagers.

The case of Qwoqwoldate

The first thing I learned about Qwoqwoldate's being a womba was that he had a collection of bones taken from bodies of persons he had eaten and that these remains were painted red. Whether they also were his victims was not clear, since the two boys (between 12 and 15 years of age at the time) who first told me about this did not specify whether the bones were from victims he had attacked and who died as a consequence of this or whether he simply ate the flesh of people who had died due to causes unrelated to him. Other opinions about this womba-man suggest, though, that the cannibalistic scenario seems more likely (discussed below).

When I asked my two young interlocutors how they knew what this womba had in his home, they said that "everybody [the villagers] says so and we heard it thus."[1] I take this and other similar statements as a collective phantasy imputation, though factually shaped to the extent that in Yagwoia mortuary practices the bones of the deceased were collected once the flesh had disintegrated and painted with red and/ or orange pigment and then disposed again, one way being interment. This would suggest that the womba-man took the bones after the corpses had already been buried and decomposed.

A mature woman and a fully initiated man told me later that Qwoqwoldate used to take and keep inside his house the skulls of deceased people, thus matching what I had already been told about the painted bones. I also learnt during a census I conducted in the lower Yalqwoyi valley where Qwoqwoldate lives that he had no garden; my assistant remarked sarcastically that his garden was dead people's skulls (*aama piye mnekna*), implying that he was eating their contents, the rotting brains—of seminal quiddity because they are of the same substance as bone marrow. As for his eating habits, the two interlocutors said that he ate anything that seemed edible: "Whatever he finds on the road he just eats." The woman averred that he ate death adders (*hiquwye*) common in the grassland area while the man claimed that he once saw Qwoqwoldate eat a *piye* (dead, literally rotting and stinking) marsupial when he and others were in Hyaqauwyaalye.

These are most telling details concerning the soul of a womba-person. To start with, Yagwoia do not eat any snakes: even mentioning such a practice provokes revulsion and the thought of eating death adders, a venomous species, adds extra gravity. One telling reason given as to

---

1. Exactly at this time one of the boys, OAp, was beginning to have shamanistic dream vision experiences and, also, the first womba dream-showings. I discuss him in detail in ch. 3.

why a person would not eat a snake, no matter how hard pressed one might be, is the nightmarish possibility that the snake might become alive inside the stomach and reemerge through the mouth. The claim that Qwoqwoldate ate a rotting marsupial merely affirms the common view (and the actual experience) of the palatability range characteristic of the appetitive sensibilities of the womba-persons who, as already indicated, prefer raw and putrid meat = human flesh over and against the cooked.

In the same conversation my male interlocutor remarked on Qwoqwoldate's bodily condition, namely that it was of late looking really good: he had fattened up and was no longer just skin and bones, as he used to be. The latter is a womba-person's signature bodily condition. The reason for Qwoqwoldate's improvement was that he was spending a lot of time at the Menyamya government station in the company of the policemen and a *didiman* (agricultural officer) stationed there who were looking after him, giving him good food and such. They also gave him a portable mattress: "You see him walking with a rolled-up mattress on his shoulder and you think, there is an *a:mi* [soldier, derived from the English word "army"], but no! It is Qwoqwoldate!" commented my interlocutor.

As to how he became a womba, another man, Hiwoye, told me that this was something Qwoqwoldate caught while he was residing among the Yangluyaqance of Wapiyaalye (a Menya-speaking group) where a woman he was going to marry was from.[2] A womba-person from that area afflicted his soul, and he became one himself. The same informant said that Qwoqwoldate was a good man but that it was his *kune umpne* (thought soul) that made him a bad person: badness thus merely pertained to his womba aspect. What is significant about this view is the clear emphasis of the moral differentiation between a person's soul (i.e., its acquired potency) as malignant agency and the rest of

2. It appears that the marriage never took place.

the person. More to the point, this and other examples indicate the relative ease with which a womba-person is tolerated within the Yagwoia social body. Hiwoye, who had experienced several womba attacks though none had an effect on him, felt no grudge against the womba-persons, including against Qwoqwoldate from whom one attack had emanated. In another instance Hiwoye warded off an attack by the soul of a womba-man from Iqumdi[3] by beating him with a burning log. Again, he knew the man and was visiting his place at the time. It should be said that when I got to know him, Qwoqwoldate did not have a family of his own and was living with his matrilateral half-sister. He had spent quite a few years as indentured laborer on the coast and the islands. The fact that he was also being looked after by such *ulyce* (outsiders) as policemen at the Menyamya station was symptomatic of his relative marginality in the context of Yagwoia sociality, yet it would be erroneous to cast his womba fixture in terms of such a position within their field of relatedness.[4]

The case of WoGaye

Another permanent Iqwaye womba, WoGaye (that is, his soul), was said to gorge exclusively on human cadaver and the putrid fluids (*piyagne*) of decomposing corpses while vomiting at the sight of good pork. He was unable to eat the kind of meat that every ordinary Yagwoia person relishes. When OMitane was telling me about this, we and all others present laughed. He asked me: "What do you think about it? He vomits at the sight of pork but eats cadaver?! Good,

---

3. The people from Iqumdi are called Yaqauwye (NW Ankave-Angan speakers); about them more in ch. 6.
4. There are other marginal individuals in Yagwoia lifeworld, but they are not, simply for that reason, alleged to be womba. My point is that every human soul is open to the womba temptations and can succumb to them.

ah?!!" OMitane himself was subject to recurrent womba dream visions to which he did not give in, no matter how overwhelming they were (see ch. 3).

Over the years I saw WoGaye only occasionally since he lived in the lower Yalqwoyi valley whereas I lived in the headwaters area and, later, over the range, in Iwolaqa-Malycaane, another Yagwoia territorial group. He had two wives and five children. Only once did I ask him directly about his womba soul-condition, which he denied rather sheepishly. By contrast even his closest agnatic relations, including his true brothers and their wives, asserted that he was a womba with the sort of peculiarity of eating only human cadavers. The common view was that this occurs solely in the context of mortuary séances (*aa:ma-ka:se*) where people spend prolonged time in the presence of the corpse of a deceased person. The spectacular bloating of the corpse and the copious oozing of cadaverous fluids that then takes place is what stimulated the womba desire of WoGaye's soul. People claimed that they saw his stomach swelling up due to the ingestion of cadaverous fluids (*ingaalye*) and he was also allegedly seen vomiting blood ingested from the corpse. One Iqwaye told me that he always gets weary when WoGaye turns up at a mortuary séance, which is why he, and perhaps some other Iqwaye, avoid sitting next to him on such occasions. Shamans treated him but with no lasting effect. However, this predicament did not deprive him of normal sociality and he lived as everybody else. I should say that WoGaye is quite a sight to behold. He has a ghastly scar across this throat, spanning both ears, caused by a self-inflicted injury when using a contraption he procured while working on a coastal plantation. Impressed by the efficiency of the scissor-like cutters used for harvesting coconuts, he tried using them at home to cut down pandanus nuts. When he tested the cutters, they broke off from the pole to which they were attached, and the lower, razor-sharp blade, which he was manipulating by means of a long string, fell down and almost decapitated him. The medical orderly in Kwaplalim did a functionally excellent if aesthetically rough job, so that the thick long scar looked like a noose lying permanently around his neck.[5]

A specifically female aspect of the womba complex

Although anyone's soul is open to the womba affliction, I never knew a Yagwoia woman whose soul suffered such a plight as the souls of the men I describe in this work.[6] As far as living memory goes, there were only two confirmed womba-women among the Iqwaye and both were killed, though not in their human embodiment. However, there is a specifically female circumscription of the womba condition, namely that relating to the cannibalistic determination of matrifiliation. In ordinary life-situations a woman may be reproached, usually by her disgruntled husband, for being a womba-*aapale* (womba-woman), as when she demands meat too often and is greedy for it. However, the most likely circumstance to occasion a reprimand such as "I think that you are a womba-woman" is when a woman loses too many children, either at birth or shortly thereafter.

---

5. According to another, albeit apocryphal, version, his near self-decapitation was caused by his predilection to innovate local, well-established cultural techniques. In this account he wanted to make the butchering of pigs easier than when the animal lies prostrate on the ground and tried to hang a pig from a tree branch by means of an iron hook tied to a rope. As he was winching the pig skyward, it slipped off the hook. The hook swinged out but, because he stood too close, slammed into him, catching him at his throat. Yet, as he was still pulling on the rope, the hook then ripped open his throat.

6. I will reflect on this in ch. 6 in the context of a comparative perspective on the womba complex.

Infant mortality among the Yagwoia is high[7] and it quickly translates into a most burdensome social predicament as the father (= husband) has to make mortuary payments to the mothers (male and female) of his dead offshoots (*uwye*). This causes two forms of self-deprivation: the man loses his progeny and therewith his self-continuation, and he has to part with his shells/money as *aamekne* (death) payment. The woman who loses too many children becomes a drain of her husband's vital bodily substance. Instead of generating a double gain through her labor (children and wealth), her body and womb siphon off her man's bone strength into the bottomless mouths and stomachs of his affines who are the mothers—the life-owners of his dead children. More often than not, after one or two dead infants a Yagwoia man will avoid making any payments if another child dies. This strains the relations with his affines who will pressure their sister/daughter, the man's wife, to express their sentiment to him, namely that he is a lousy affine. This in turn will anger him, and it is during such altercations that a man may accuse his wife of being a womba-woman who eats her own children and makes his life miserable. This sort of verbal castigation has a distinctive existential meaning-force precisely because Yagwoia mothers do—albeit in a culturally symbolic-sublimated mode—eat their children. Let me elaborate this.

After being born, every Yagwoia neonate—whose kinesthetic torpidity still projects the dynamism of its primal, maternal womb-container—is rubbed with yellow ochre and marsupial grease to make its flesh consubstantial

---

7. A woman who wishes to effectively dissolve her marital relation may also resort to deliberate infanticide, which will prompt her man to get rid of her. A man (as well as other consociates) is likely to suspect his woman of doing this if their everyday relations are fraught with quarrels and, especially, if she happened to have liked another man but got "taken" by (i.e., married to) a man she dislikes.

with its macrocosmic elementality of the world-body, the earth substance.[8] Male or female, each neonate is thus born and identified as a marsupial correlative of the real marsupials that were hunted by the father (and/or his co-initiates or, in case the father is absent, his WB, the neonate's maternal uncle) and given to a group of women for consumption. More explicitly, in this paternal frame of the neonate = marsupial delivery, the neonate = marsupial is hunted = shot = killed = procreated by the father and as such (multiplied) is given to the *actual* mother as well as to her and his (father's) classificatory mothers. Thus, with the exception of the neonate's mother, all these recipient women are the neonate's parents' classificatory mothers and grandmothers. These women eat the marsupials that, being identical with the newborn, are its obviative substitute. That is why the neonate is smeared with the marsupial grease (as is its mother) and, regardless of its sexedness, a pendant composed of dry marsupial testicles and one or two bones (representing the penis) is attached to its postpartum womb-container, the net-bag. No man partakes of the childbirth marsupials, but in the context of male initiation ceremonies an equivalent distribution of marsupial meat takes place among men.

The scene of a *hiye malaye* (childbirth marsupial) distribution is most exciting: marsupials, piled high in the uncovered stone oven, are cooking and fuming, surrounded by women of all ages, some pregnant with little "marsupials" gestating in their wombs, others suckling the "marsupials"

---

8. For a more detailed presentation of the *hiye malaye* (childbirth marsupial) practice, see Mimica (1981: 111–14; 1991: 90–92). The identification neonate = marsupial derives from the cosmogonic process where the first human neonate (Red Man), born out of the first woman's phallic womb, appeared as a marsupial (Mimica 1981). This identity is subject to further articulation in the five male initiations, various contexts of everyday life, and verbal expressions.

already born. All are happy. "Aiiiy! The *hiye malaye* tastes sweet!" The women—a gathering of G/Mothers[9]—"eat back" that which came out of their bodies. Indeed, Yagwoia mothers (male and female) are indissolubly bound to their children by the dynamic bonds of relatedness qua eating. Through a series of life-cycle payments/prestations, a person's mother eats back her child repeatedly, in life and in death (thus through mortuary payment): what used to be inside her womb goes back from the outside into the inside once parturition has occurred (for details, see Mimica 1991).

But every eaten is also an eater, so that a mother is herself being eaten, both in utero (in gestation) and postpartum (through breastfeeding). The Yagwoia, quite correctly, see the infant's bodily life (growth) for what it is: a cannibalistic process in which the infant eats the mother's bodily substance; all the care and work that goes into child-rearing is duly acknowledged by men and women alike to be hard work that drains the mother's body. Woman's maternal labor in its pregnant sense is the basis of the life-cycle payments to every person's mothers (male and female). The primordial conjunction of the mouth and the breast-nipple establishes a closed circuit that at once continues and transfigures the primal intrauterine one that in the Yagwoia lifeworld has the determination I call phallo-umbilical (Mimica 1991).

The Yagwoia bodily milieu of the mouth-breast, on the whole, has a veneer of opulence. What I mean by this is not so much the empirical availability of maternal milk, for many a woman may lactate poorly, but the availability of the breast regardless of its lacteal power. Yagwoia infants are minimally deprived of what truly is their proper self-object. Breast is virtually always made available. In many instances the volume of the breast and the size of the infant's body closely approximate each other. Even when obstructed by

---

9. I use this specification (G = grand-kin) in order to foreground the "mother" category in this class of female grand-kin.

blouses and textile clothes, which figure as regular items of attire worn either permanently or occasionally, most women will readily allow their ambulatory infants to have access to their breasts, for that is their fundamental determination in the Yagwoia lifeworld. They are coextensive with the child. In its demands, the child is often whimsical, and a momentary oral-mammary conjunction will quickly cease only to be resumed a few moments later. In such engagements the Yagwoia mother will most likely interrupt her activities in order to accommodate the child's whim.[10]

Both women and men have a firm view that there is a pronounced difference between male and female children concerning the attachment to the breast and the weaning age. On the basis of my observations, I believe that this opinion is quite accurate. Thus in the view of Yagwoia mothers in particular, male children generally tend to breastfeed longer (five to six years) than female children, the latter already abandoning the breast in average between two-and-a-half and three years of age. Girls also tend to let go much more easily and spontaneously while boys may have to be forced to do so. For this purpose, the mother will smear her nipples with an extraction from what I believe to be a capsicum species. The juice tastes hot and acidy, giving the breastfeeding boy a nasty surprise—one may say a mammary-grenade bursting in his mouth. It may take no more than two or three such experiences to bring the boy's oral-mammary paradise to a painful and terminal closure.

---

10. It should be mentioned that breastfeeding in its core has an aspect of work-for-life. Heimann (1962: 412) aptly observed that "the sucking infant in his blissful experience at the breast is also *working* for his living seems little acknowledged in the literature....In contrast to the pattern of work laid down by the feeding experience at the mother's breast, and later continued when the child learns to speak, the work pattern derived from the anal stage demands withdrawal from the community and loneliness and full autonomy in the productive act."

However, it is not often that such a traumatic weaning procedure has to be used and it would thus be biased to frame it as a source of "oral frustration due to weaning" and considering it an influential component in the formation of the Yagwoia womba complex.[11]

This, then, is the positive cultural core-cannibalistic milieu that underpins the negative notion of the woman as a mother = womba-*aapale* who devours her children. It also resonates negatively in a number of unfortunate happenings. In the center of every Yagwoia domestic space is an open fire-hearth, and both children and adults risk suffering severe, sometimes deadly burns. Reflecting the cosmo-ontological significance of the child's being, it is said

---

11. In this connection a comment is necessary on the relation between the womba complex and the historical changes in, and eventual collapse of, the initiation system. The fundamental issue in this regard is that the net effect of these changes is the erosion and collapse of the transmission and inculcation of a whole range of values constitutive of the Yagwoia male ethos and self-conduct, whose correlate is a specific configuration of the super-ego structuration. But this does not translate into a specifically determining effect on the womba complex. I stress this precisely because well before the final collapse of the initiation system the absence of the fellatio practice had certainly affected the de facto phallo-umbilical incorporative experience (which was the substitutive continuation of breastfeeding) of all the generations of men thus initiated. Nevertheless, the oral incorporative desire, intrinsic to the womba complex, remains no matter what since breastfeeding and correlative orally calibrated desire are universal, regardless of how problematic the access to the breast may be. Fellatio was but a modal and historically contingent expression of that nuclear drive and desire as is the womba complex itself. More to the point, the Yagwoia's neighbors, the Paṭaye (Menya) and Ankave, are subject to variants of the womba complex, but institutionalized homosexuality was never a component of their initiation systems (see ch. 6).

of a burnt child that its mother must have thought it was a marsupial rather than her child, so she let go of it and in return got herself a roasted marsupial. I first heard this sort of remark when I saw a child being treated for burns at a Yagwoia aid post in Kwaplalim.[12]

Womba killing

I know of only two cases of womba killing among the Yagwoia. One took place, most likely, in the mid-to-late 1940s and the other in 1977, just before I started my fieldwork. In both instances the persons were women (hence womba-*aapale*) but—and here is the crucial aspect of these incidents—*they were not apprehended and killed in their human embodiment but in the embodiment of a pig*. Both cases are virtually identical so I will summarize the

---

12. The late Tom Ernst made a somewhat parallel observation for the Onabasulu people of Mount Bosavi (personal communication). During his first fieldwork he was accompanied by his wife and young daughter. The girl, around five years old, very quickly became assimilated into the local milieu, including learning the vernacular. On one occasion a local girl fell into a fire and was badly burnt. Her relatives brought her to Tom and his wife, a qualified nurse, for treatment. As they attended to the little girl Tom's daughter, who was highly attuned to the cannibalistic dimension of Onabasulu intersubjectivity, told her father to check if the girl might not have been deliberately thrown into fire in order to be eaten. Startled by his daughter's request Tom dismissed it, whereupon she told him: "You! Don't you know that they eat people here!" Without excluding the probability that her own cannibalistic phantasies may also be at play (since these are common in childhood, irrespective of how salient they may be in a given cultural reality; see, for instance, Bloch 1978), the ethnographer's daughter was astutely cued into the Onabasulu cultural reality. For a scholarly account of Onabasulu cannibalism, see Ernst (1999).

more recent one, the account of which I obtained from Katasaqulyi, one of the two young men involved in the killing. In 1977 Katasaqulyi and the other young man were *qwomalye takayine* (nose-pierced boys, thus first stage initiates) in their mid-teens. There was a pig that, time and time again, broke into his sister's garden located on the fringes of the forest. It always happened at night so that he and his *katouqwa* (co-initiate), accompanied by the latter's father's younger brother (FB = F), decided to keep a watch one moonlit night. Sure enough they saw a pig breaking through the fence. They shot three arrows, of which at least one hit the pig, which ran away. They followed the pig, but she[13] disappeared. In the morning Katasaqulyi's sister went to urinate near the garden when she spotted a pig sitting as if it were a human person with her back resting against a tree. She came back to the garden house and reported this to the two teenagers and their elder companion. The three went off in pursuit of this strange pig, now suspecting it to be a womba because she was seen sitting like a human person.

The three first came across the pig's footprints, leading to a garden whose owner they knew. This was later seen as a deliberate maneuver by the pig, to fool the pursuers and everybody else into thinking that she was shot at that place. But the tracks continued to the footpath where they found vomited blood and pieces of the sweet potato she

---

13. I am using the third female pronoun not just because this pig, as it turned out, was a womba-woman but because in the Yagwoia lifeworld, unless it is explicitly specified that the animal in question is a boar, a pig is categorically female. The most trenchant statement to this effect is made in the context of the initiation ceremonies when initiates are told that every man's first woman is a proper pig and only qua her, that is, through the exchange of pork for shells/money, can one procure the other (human) woman with whom he copulates and makes children (see ch. 5) .

had ransacked from their garden. When they continued following the footprints, they found that the pig's footprints turned into human ones at place X; and when they followed these, they were surprised to find, at place Y, they turned into a dog's footprints, only to turn back into human prints at place Z.

At the fence near the house of NGy-Ca'paqulyi, a local man, they again found vomited blood and pieces of sweet potato. They now decided that this must be the pig's house. They thus entered the homestead and asked NGy-Ca'paqulyi: "Whose pig was the one that went there?" Perplexed he said that he had seen no pig and that there was no-one inside the homestead. They told him that they had followed a trail of blood and sweet potato vomit, and that the footprints had changed three times: from pig to human to dog and back to human. In Kaṯasaqulyi's account the husband began to think that this might well be the work of his Yaqauwye woman whom he had obtained cheaply and, by and large, did not really care about; she thus was, as the Yagwoia say, an unguarded garden whose fence was broken by numerous men.[14] NGy-Ca'paqulyi also knew that Yaqauwye people are invariably all womba (see ch. 6). So when he, his first wife (of four), and the pursuers went to check inside the house, they found his Yaqauwye woman lying on the floor, groaning and complaining about the pain in her vital organs (collectively called *qalye*, principally the heart, lungs, and liver): "Oooh, my *qalye* is pain-doing [aching] me" (*ngalye qalye ise nyinatana*). When NGy-Ca'paqulyi and the first wife asked her about her pain, she did not respond; instead she vomited blood and pieces of semi-digested sweet potato and *pitpit*.[15] "We all saw that,"

---

14. The characterization "promiscuous" follows the account of my Yagwoia informants that in this regard represents the woman in terms of a general image of women's sexual desire and the fact that both men and women do pursue extramarital sex.

15. *Pitpit* refers to a range of species/varietals of edible grass.

said the narrator. She died that same afternoon. When the pursuers who, in the meantime, had returned to their garden homestead heard of this, they commented to the effect that "she has got what she deserved" because all the time she, in her pig embodiment, had been damaging not just their garden but many other gardens, thereby enticing other pigs to do the same.

Several aspects of this incident must be highlighted. First, only in the aftermath of the woman's death was her womba identity ascertained and, accordingly, the responsibility for the killing affirmed. By the same token, the two boys and their older guardian were worried that for that very reason they might be held liable and taken to court. A local *komiti* (local government councillor) determined, however, that there was no basis for any court hearing and adjudication as it had not been a human person (that is, in the human embodiment) who was ruining gardens and stealing sweet potatoes and then got shot (a fact that would make it a case for the court) but a womba-woman's *umpne* that had turned into a pig. They had no need to worry. Moreover, some other people's gardens were also damaged by this pig = womba-woman who was enticing other pigs into doing the same mischief. Now that she had been shot, all gardens were safe and they had done a good thing. There was also some apprehension that her people, well known for their deadly brand of sorcery, might retaliate, but nothing of the sort ensued.

NGy-Ca'paqulyi, the woman's husband, made no argument against the *komiti's* reasoning; since she was a Yaqauwye woman from Iqumdi, she was a marginal outsider in the Iqwaye abode. He was concerned, however, that her relatives from Yaqauwyaane might come to claim *aa'mekne* (mortuary payment), so that he kept quiet, to avoid such an eventuality no matter what. It was in reference to this case that I heard an opinion as to why the Iqwaye (and other Yagwoia) *do not kill* womba-persons in their human embodiment: doing so would entail paying compensation.

A human life qua human bodily form belongs to those who brought it into existence, one's mothers, and as such has an irreducible value that requires appropriate recompense. But when, as in this case, a womba-person's soul turns into a pig, this precept has little weight.

The second aspect of this (and the related) case is the womba-woman's porcine behavior. There is a latent meaning underpinning the overt behavior of this *one* pig that was enticing *many other* pigs *to break into so many gardens and eat* sweet potato. In her human form the Yaqauwye woman was promiscuous: *many men* penetrated her, that is, *broke her fence* and planted their semen. As a pig she was, as it were, doing the same by bringing into so many gardens a plurality of other pigs that rummaged the food growing in there. The metaphoric transposition involves one^many inversions and pivots on the ouroboric equivalence between genital and oral sex: copulation = eating (see Mimica 1981, 1991). This is indicative of the intersubjective dynamics of the phantasy formation pivoting on the culturally salient woman = pig identification.[16] From it follows another implication, namely the reported fact that, as a pig, this womba-woman did not eat human flesh or, let alone, attack other pigs, whereas a womba-person's soul does. Although I obtained no comment on this I see it as a symptomatic expression of the inner logic of this complex in relation to the overall libidinal dynamics of desire articulated in the primary modality of the self-world relationship, eating and food.

Regarding this case, let me amplify the way the blending of empirical-perceptual and phantasy dynamics generates its latent transfiguration. The empirically overt manifestation of this woman's womba soul was that she appeared as a pig and—as the canine footprints indicated—a dog. But of the two animal forms it is the porcine that was perceptually

---

16. In fact, the full nexus is woman = pig = mother/breast = wealth (see ch. 4).

experientially and maximally real since the woman was apprehended and shot in that form; her canine form was manifest solely as footprints, that is, as a metonymic trace, so to speak. In the pig form, then, her womba-hood expressed itself in the faithful mode of the porcine (animal) behavior: breaking into gardens and eating sweet potatoes. The implication is that, although being a womba, such a soul may cease to be motivated by the human-cannibalistic desire and turn, so to speak, radically allo-phageous: eating no flesh of whatever kind and state but only tubers. Considered within the purview of the dynamics of the wider spectrum of Yagwoia cannibalism (more in ch. 4) and their cultural imaginary, this observation can be expressed in the following formulation: in its porcine, that is, female, embodiment the womba complex seems to reach its dialectical self-fulfillment, thereby producing its self-other alimentary auto-alteration, thus turning into its self-opposite. As a corporeal pig (= woman), the soul has literally fulfilled its craving for human = porcine flesh and thus achieved its full incorporative, thus autophagous, identification with the object of desire. Then follows a dialectical self-negating or self-differentiating effect, one that can also be thought of as a sort of chiasmus: the soul renders itself allo-phageous, and the pig prefers to eat its proper allo-substance, tubers, although, as the Yagwoia know only too well, they eat worms and, given the opportunity, a human being as well.

CHAPTER 3

Womba self-experience

I now turn to the primary dimension of the womba complex, the actual self (soul)-experience that occurs in menacing dreams and dream-generated wakeful visions (hallucinations in our frame of self-understanding). In other words, I am seeking the locus of womba reality not as function of what is said about it in reference to those who are claimed to be womba but rather as what that condition is like as a lived actuality one is subjected to.

The case of OMitane

Earlier I mentioned OMitane who laughed while commenting on WoGaye's womba predicament to the effect that he eats human cadaver but is repelled to the point of vomiting by the sight of good pork. OMitane was truly a superlative man of yore: he had in all five women, with four of whom he had no less than twenty-four children. Three died while still young. The remaining twenty-one comprised nine daughters and thirteen sons. Of the latter, seven became fully initiated in the 1973–80 initiation cycle. In addition, OMitane took paternal care of two boys and one girl by his third and fourth wives' previous men. His fifth woman was his lifelong adulterous lover who was married to OMaica, his much older *amnelyi* (classificatory matrilateral brother).

It was a fait accompli that she would go to OMitane when her husband died. And so she did when the time came, to everyone's approval and satisfaction, including OMitane's other wives. OMitane also obtained his third and fourth wives through matrilateral levirate. The third, Nguyipu, was also OMitane's classificatory FM (*kate*), thus from the same *latice*[1] as his FM and so the conduit of the *caqamnene* (replacement) whereby her children, specifically her sons, came to replace his father both in name and fullness of their corporeality (bone and flesh).[2] She became and remained his favorite woman until the end of his life. This was manifestly the case since he almost always slept in her house.

OMitane was a hardworking polygamist who knew well how to keep his polygamous household optimally viable. At his village homestead, each wife had her own sleeping hut and

---

1. *Latice* is a common vernacular label for Yagwoia social groups. It can be glossed as "clans," but at the price of undue distortions. The word refers to intra-bodily "knots" or "vital centers" in which are conjoined intra-skeletal passages through which circulates bone marrow. These are located at various junctions, especially along the spine. In Yagwoia understanding, marrow is the source of semen (in men) and breast milk (in women). The uppermost vital knot is at the occipital point of the skull and the lower-most one lies in the groin. The latter is the last station through which bone marrow flows into the penis. It is specifically this penile *latice* (the "root knot") that is intended when used as a generic term for Yagwoia social units that are the framework of their naming system (see Mimica 1981; 1988; 1991; 2006: 32–37). In parallel with the bone marrow (= seminal/lacteal) intra-skeletal passages and their knots, there is a second set of *latice* knots that bind all the *mdjace une* (blood-ropes, or, in Western terms, veins and arteries, between which the Yagwoia do not differentiate).

2. For the logic of this full identity replication (bodily and nominal) in alternate generations (FF=SS) effected by a man marrying his classificatory FM, see Mimica (1991: 87–90).

there were three separate cooking houses. That is, each had her own domestic turf not shared with any other co-wife. Thus, their residence was most of the time equilibrated through a maximal separation. In Iqwaye perception OMitane was not just good at managing his women well, for by and large their relations were without conflict, but also at keeping an eye on them so that, with only a few exceptions, no other man dared "to venture into his gardens," that is, attempt adultery with his women. By managing to prevent other men from vicariously penis-shooting him (to use the literal gloss)[3] and thus being "on top" of him, he was able to assert his dominance over them, elevating his phallic egoity to even higher levels. Whether due to envy or a positive desire to have sex with him, men and women alike recognized and acknowledged his supreme bone-strength; and men would not dare challenge him for most were no match to him when it came to fighting. OMitane, however, never succumbed to a whimsical abuse of his personal power against his fellow villagers, nor did he transform it into the kind of prestige that, for instance, his old father wielded. As his fighting career ended with the cessation of warfare under the Pax Australiana (ca. 1955–63), he continued to accomplish himself through prolific self-implantation, by siring so many children, and industriousness. But the legacy of his achievements as a warrior-killer—in all he killed some ten people—was a distinctive mark of his status as a vintage *aamnye neima'nye* (big man) of yore. In this respect, he and two of his *katouqwa* (co-initiates)—who each killed about a dozen people while still bound to *hiqwona* (the bachelors' hut, thus while they were still young bachelors)—

---

3. This literal translation captures the way in which the act of copulation is verbalized in Yagwoia. It is formed from the same verb stem as arrow shooting. The two actions are differentiated by the use of different nouns that specify the instruments (agents) of the action in question, thus the *lakice* (penis) for copulation and the *mace* (arrow) for shooting. Both male and female speakers use this formulation.

epitomized the sort of bone-power that the post-pacification generations of Yagwoia men could no longer hope to either master or display.

OMitane used to trade in salt and tapa with the Yaqauwye (NW Ankave) and it was they who afflicted his soul. As far as my knowledge of his womba predicament goes it was during the 1980s that he began to experience frequent womba dream-showings of hallucinatory intensity. I characterize them so because when he talked to me about them, he insisted that he was not asleep but wide awake, watching ghastly spectacles dominated by butchered pigs. This made him jump and fall over Nguyipu in whose hut he liked to sleep. His young uninitiated teenage (*qwomalye*) sons confirmed his behavior, adding that they did not like to sleep in his company because of this.[4] The following is a summary of one such experience from 1985:

> OMitane woke up screaming and trampling his old woman (his third wife) who got up to fetch some *ilyqalye* (an aromatic plant). She lit a piece of tapa and, holding this and the *ilyqalye*, encircled him by moving her hand around his body. The scent and smoke created a protective envelope against the assaulting spirit(s) (*ilymane*); this allowed him to compose himself. OMitane was now fully awake and sitting upright, but the experience continued. He saw his daughter (by his first wife) come inside the house and sit down close to him. He saw her thus but realized with a start that it was not her physical self but her soul (*kune umpne*), bearing her semblance. He then saw one of his pigs being sliced open lengthwise along its belly with a Singer knife (a machete). One side cleaved open completely yet remained attached to the other half which, in turn, stayed upright so that he could see all its entrails and

---

4. OMitane's sons were present in my hut when he gave me his account. One of them was OAp who is discussed below.

vital organs (*qalye*). The pig did not die but kept on moving. Another pig appeared, also cut open, though not lengthwise like the first pig but front-back, with the torso cleaved close to the back legs.

Then men appeared. He started grabbing them one by one, but as he did so their bones crumbled (a sure sign that these were spirits in human semblance). Next his daughter's son (DS) YaOmaqwa (a young boy at the time) and OWiyanye, OMitane's classificatory agnatic brother and co-initiate (and shaman) appeared. YaOmaqwa used his hand like a knife to cut OWiyanye's nose. OWiyanye groaned—aargh—and blood shot out, red like the juice of the *hyamane* (red pandanus) and *nakiye* (betel nut). OMitane then took some banana skin (i.e., soft bark) and used it to clean OWiyanye's nose and plug his mouth (presumably to stop bleeding). Then he watched OWiyanye go.

I will restrict myself to only a few comments on the manifest content. First is the symptomatic pattern of the pig imagery, which reflects the geometrical characteristic of the Yagwoia style of butchering a pig (see ch. 4). However, in the dream vision this is articulated as an acute expression of the womba perspective on embodiment whereby the body (porcine or human) is at once penetrated (and in a sense opened up) and conserved. It is at once living and dead. In this particular vision OMitane makes no contact with the pig flesh—he *does not eat it*. His sole destructive conjunction is with the semblance of men whose limbs he breaks; but he spills no blood.[5] The culturally salient act of castration is committed by OMitane's DS who bloodies the (pierced) nose of OMitane's agnate. The nose is the most untouchable part of a man's libidinal embodiment, a

---

5. A variant of this motif occurs in the onset experiences leading to the acquisition of healing soul-powers, including the power to set broken bones.

phallic-bisexual nucleus created as such in the first initiation ceremony. No matter how expressive this vision is of the aggressive effluence of OMitane's (un)conscious, it is his grandson, a noninitiated boy, who manifests the violence while he, a consummate warrior-killer of yore, attends to the wounds of his bloodied agnate and co-initiate. However, the grand-kin relation between a man and his DS is one of mutual identity: a daughter's children are always referred to in reference to their mother's father (the maternal GF). Thus, the DS whom OMitane sees in the dream would be known as YaOmaqwa OMitane *kayeqwa* (literally YaOmaqwa OMitane 3S-grand-kin-male, or YaOmaqwa whose maternal GF is OMitane). Finally, it is significant that it was his daughter's soul rather than, say, that of one of his sons who sat next to him in the wake of the spectacle. This is indicative of the saliency of the bond between father and daughter in the Yagwoia lifeworld.

As so many times before, after this particular experience OMitane told other men about the showing (*ucoqwalye*) that had befallen him. Their answer was predictable: he should ask HCapalyi, his DH and a well-known shaman, to cast out the *ilymane* responsible for these recurrent showings. The fact is that OMitane had done so many times before but each time, after a short period during which everything was fine, the showings came back anew. Such was the case with his womba complex: recurrent menacing showings that did not corrupt his soul to such a degree that he himself became a womba.

The case of OAp

It is useful to compare the case of OMitane with that of his son OAp who, of all of OMitane's sons, was most akin to his father, specifically in regard to his sexual self-pursuit. OAp was having both the womba and the shamanistic onset experiences. The latter started early in his childhood while the former appear to have begun in his mid-teens and very possibly were influenced by his father's predicament, as one shaman also suggested. OAp's shamanistic experiences were quite persistent, but he was reticent to commit himself to them despite the fact that the wild forest spirits favored him. The reason for his hesitation was that, in his own words, "shamans deal with sickness and, therefore, you yourself may get sick." At the same time, he was gratified by these experiences.

Unlike his seven older brothers, OAp was not nose-pierced (initiated) and, consequently, his soul was not broken in and thereby directed toward the traditional course of development. In the late 1980s, he began to follow the Christian way, as taught by a resident native Lutheran catechist, and, most impressively, taught himself to read. It was in this period that many uninitiated Yagwoia adolescents of his cohort self-consciously began to pursue Christian ways and denounce the traditional *himace* (power objects) and initiations. There is no question that OAp's investment in Christianity was intense and sincere, but this has to be understood in terms of his concerns and life-situation as a person constituted in the total milieu of Yagwoia intersubjectivity. That is to say, "Christianity" here is a gloss for a horizon of existential concerns and notions that entirely belong to the Yagwoia lifeworld and its constitutive cosmo-ontological imaginal matrix. In this regard, one of the most intense concerns for OAp was with the location of that place called "Heaven" and its correlate "Paradise." The issue that preoccupied him was: "Where is this place '*Haijven*'?" I deal with this and related aspects of Yagwoia self-Christianization in a separate work. Here I want to point out that OAp was using his Christian self-pursuit as an important modus operandi against his father with whom he and his other brothers were in a prolonged conflict, harboring, as they did, a desire to kill him.[6]

---

6. See Mimica (2007b, 2010a) for discussions of the structural dynamics of the Yagwoia nuclear (oedipal) complex and kinship system.

In April 1992 OAp had a womba dream with a most acute manifest imagery; it was also the period when his sexual pursuits began to dominate his life and, by the same token, his self-Christianization began to lose its grip.

> In the dream I saw thus: OA2 (his elder second-born brother) cut off the head of a man with a machete. [He named a man whom we both knew].[7] The head fell down to one side, the body to another. OA2 cut a piece of flesh from the neck and throat that he ate; then he cut another piece and gave it to me and I ate this pig—man.[8]
>
> Then I went to a place where I saw many men killing and cooking a pig. They told me: "Eat some of this pig." But I replied: "I already ate some pig, so you just give me a little bit." "True, ah!? You are not lying?!" they said. I said: "Yes, just give me a little bit." [He did not see their faces, thus did not know who they were.] They gave me and I ate it. Then I woke up in sweat, shaken up—frightened.

Awake, he reflected on the dream and immediately realized that it was a womba dream, for he had many such showings before. A short while later he told Qang (his classificatory "mother's breast") and OT (his close agnate, FFBS = F) what he dreamt. They commended him on doing so because divulging such a dream-showing prevents it from settling in his soul. When OAp related this dream to me, Hya-Yonya, a shaman who was also present at the

---

7. The man was from Iwolaqa-Malycaane where OAp was at the time he had the dream, but the places in the dream were from OAp's home village of Yalqwaalye. There was no quarrel or fight leading up to the beheading; OAp's brother just did it. It specifically took place at their father's homestead.

8. This was a momentary yet pregnant slip as the next development in the dream shows.

time, reiterated this view. To the extent that this experience stimulates and tempts the appetitive desire that can make the dreamer succumb to it and develop the cannibalistic taste and craving, OAp stated that he "didn't like the taste of the human flesh; it was the same as the pig-fat [*quwace*] and it spoiled my throat [was unpalatable]." This negative valorization of pig-fat is commonly asserted by Yagwoia who do not like pig-fat but greatly valorize the proper pig-meat (*nguce*). Although in the dream he shows some restraint when offered more pig-meat—he asks for just "a little bit"—the force of his cannibalistic desire is, nonetheless, manifest. Its overt vehicle is pig-meat, both as actual cooked pork and as a slip of the tongue. In fact, the differentiation between the two is of no consequence. In either manifestation, the object of desire and its drive are transparently oral-cannibalistic.

Importantly, throughout the dream his position is passive and receptive; the decapitation was executed by his older brother who also gives him the flesh. Similarly, it is other men who killed the pig and offered him some while he, at the receiving end, duly ate it. However, the agentive saliency of his brother is not to be seen in opposition to OAp's passive-receptive stance: they share the substantial bodily identity (same patri-bone and maternal bodily flesh-envelope), which as such is embedded in their names. The sole nominal difference lies in their birth-order suffixes: OA2 is *aqulyi* (second-born) while OAp is *pacoqwa* (fourth-born). In this respect it can be said that OA2 carries OAp's full identity to a maximal degree—he is his doppelgänger. However, precisely because they are so fully the same, the Yagwoia view same-sex full male siblings as intrinsically predisposed to mutual antagonism, which comes to the fore in relation to their sister(s)'s bride-price and land inheritance. On the other hand, in the Yagwoia view it is a man's classificatory matrilateral brother—the same bodily flesh = matri-name but not the same patri-name = bones (i.e., of a different *latice* group)—who is of a genuinely amicable disposition. And when such a brother figures in a dream, it is he who is the salient manifestation of the dreamer's identity—his maternal flesh—and as such is truly his doppelgänger, an unambiguous self, so that whatever he does also applies to the dreamer. In this respect, when applied to OMitane's dream-showing, the latter's identity with his DS has a greater self-symmetry than the identity of OAp and OA2. Accordingly, it can be said that, in terms of agentivity, there is a greater equivalence between OMitane and his DS than between OAp and his brother, although both are in a manifestly passive position vis-à-vis the violent activity unfolding in their dreams.

I should also point out that OAp's dream relates to a wakeful life-situation in which the dreamer and his brothers were involved in a physical confrontation with their father during a pig kill when the distribution of the pork went awry. Without going into any detail I can say that this actual event and the dreamer's life-situation, in which the conflict was an eruptive climax, are refracted and synthesized through the prism of OAp's womba dream that he had exactly at the time when he gave me the account of the conflict between the brothers and their father. The manifest imagery in his dream situation relates to or resonates with the actual situation of the conflict. Where in the dream it is his elder brother OA2 who decapitates a man, in the actual conflict OA2's forehead was cut by OMitane's machete—the turning point in the bust-up with his sons. In both situations the event took place at his father's homestead. In the second dream-scene OAp comes to another place where a pig was offered to him. In the situation of his wakeful lifeworld, both the beginning and the end of the conflict were mediated by the carving up and eventual consumption of a pig, which assuaged the conflict; the former was frustrated but in the latter context OAp was altogether left out, which made him resentful.

In our conversation OAp also retailed how, long before this dream, when he was still a boy, he used to see this sort of showing: they (people in the dream) would kill a huge pig and then would give him some to eat. Significantly, he also dreamt of his father OMitane giving him pig-meat. He went on dream-seeing this, but eventually he talked it out because he got worried that he would become a womba-boy.

Regardless, these dream-showings continued. Then OAp had a particularly alarming one in which he himself killed a big pig and ate it. Some of the meat was stinking because it was putrid (in the dream he smelt its *piyagne* [stench]), yet some was raw, and some cooked. He woke up distressed and enraged by the experience, so much that he broke through the wall of the hut in which he was sleeping, shouting: "What is this dream that I see all the time?!" The other boys who also slept there woke up and asked what was going on and why he had broken the house. He told them of the dream. The angry act of breaking the wall, one can characterize it as a remonstration with his soul, had a lasting effect—"After this I didn't see it again. I cast off this womba and I saw it no more"—because he really *did not want it*. What comes to the fore in this dream and its aftermath is that throughout OAp is an active agent: he himself kills the pig and eats it. This stands in contrast to his previous dreams where he was always and only the recipient. It is clear enough that this intra-oneiric active agency carried on into wakefulness where his forceful willful act effectively broke off the titillation of *his* cannibalistic desire and so he was freed of it until now, when the anonymous womba has returned.

I remarked to OAp that this showing was the womba's last challenge to him: before this one, he was (only) eating pig-meat; now he ate (undisguised) human flesh. Nevertheless, I indicated, he could overpower this womba as he did before and route it completely. I said this to encourage him, even as I had the impression that he felt quite self-assured about it and for a good reason: he had successfully dealt with his womba vicissitudes in the past, more or less on his own—without the help of any shaman. Moreover, from an early age his soul had been well habituated to the realm of spirits and their powers, as in parallel to the malignant womba showings he had been exposed to shamanistic visions. OAp's egoity and his soul could thus draw on an acquaintance with the powers of the local spiritual *Umwelt* (the collective cultural imaginary in our terms) in order to cope with and parry its malignant agencies. In view of my knowledge of OAp's life in the years subsequent to this particular dream-showing, I came to conclude that he was content to live with the cannibalistic malignancy of his soul in correlation with his steady sexual success. The latter included acquiring his first wife, the decline of his self-Christianization and, most importantly, his and his brothers' ascendancy over their father OMitane.[9]

In subsequent reports on his womba dream-showings (from 1994 onward), the following developments took place. His active murderous cannibalistic sense of agency became crystalized, for in the dream-showings it was he who was actually killing a man, commonly by cutting his throat (*a:qoce*), and eating the latter.[10] All of the men he ate were grown-ups. On one intra-oneiric occasion, after he ate a man's throat, a foul smell and taste filled his mouth; he experienced this while still dream-seeing, that is, in the dreaming sleep state. From the mid-1990s onwards

---

9. I forego a presentation of OAp's self-Christianization and the relation of his womba complex to his nuclear (pre)Oedipal complex and the overall libidinal development. Reflecting on this patrifilial kernel of the Yagwoia developmental trajectory, the sexual and womba aspects of his soul and egoity illuminate further the depth and intensity of his incorporation of his father's bone (on this process, see Mimica 2007b, 2010a).

10. I here go without a discussion of the theme of castration implicit in this motif as a phallic speech organ. This entails the presentation of Yagwoia notions of oral anatomy, speaking activity, and its development, including such soul-powers as the ability for singing.

his father's womba soul became more readily identified in the dreams. This explicitness was conterminous with the escalating conflict between father and sons. Indeed, in many of the dream-showings it was his father who would kill a pig, sometimes an enormous one, and give it to him to eat but, significantly, OAp would repel him: he would not eat it. As he explained: "He [father] is a womba and he would force it [pig] on me, but I repelled this bad spirit of his." A somewhat modified variant of this was the showings in which unknown men would give him pig-meat, which he identified in the same breath as human flesh. Here, clearly, he is placed in the passive-receptive position. On one occasion, there was just one man and he kept on pushing the pig on him, to the point that he grabbed OAp's head and forced the pig into his mouth, saying as he did so: "You eat this pig!" But OAp resisted, saying that he was weary of eating "this pig of yours!" He repelled the pig with such force in fact that he woke up, overwhelmed by such anger that, like in the earlier dream, he smashed the wall of the hut in which he was sleeping.

What is manifest in his showings is OAp's ambivalence: on the one hand, he was literally consummating the womba desire of his soul, for he was doing his own killing and eating pig = human flesh; on the other hand, however, when this desire was mediated by other presences, including that of his father, he passionately resisted it. There was a clear fissure and tension in the phallo-oral (ouroboric) core of his soul and the identity of the agency of his immanent self-otherness was sliding from known presences (including that of his father) to unknown presences: this is symptomatic of the dynamics of the super-ego formation in the field of Yagwoia intersubjectivity. It will suffice to highlight that the paternal presence in the ouroboric super-ego constellation is subordinate to the primary maternal core.

Reflecting on the psycho-dynamic implications of the difference between OAp and his father in the manifest content of their womba showings, it is obvious that OMitane is in passive subjection to them, and no overt (undisguised) cannibalistic imagery is in evidence. This is symptomatic of OMitane's attenuated aggressive-destructive drive-circuitry that was fully consummated in actual practice when, early on in his life, he accomplished himself as a spectacular killer. In regard to his sexual pursuits, which continued virtually to his death, he remained "on the top" of all other men—undefeated. In this respect, it can be said that his *libido dominandi* was maximally ego-syntonic while in the domain of womba showings there was no sufficient inner motivation in his soul to mount a forceful repulsion. This would have probably generated a different kind of showing. The situation for his son OAp was different. Uninitiated and with a lifeworld that no longer offered the arena for destruction of human life and correlative self-consummation as a warrior-killer (which is a mode of generative effluence qua destruction, i.e., libido turns into extreme aggression = destrudo), OAp's womba situation seems more ego-syntonic, both with respect to his oedipal struggle and the self-affirmation as the vanquisher of men. As he said, all of his victims were "grown-ups," thus mature men, hence the progression of his showings from passive subjection to active cannibalism.[11]

---

11. Overall, one can discern in the concrete womba showings (i.e., phantasy productions that as such manifest the real passions of the soul) a range of variations along the passivity^activity cline indicative of, if only implicitly, the biographical experience of life^death that shapes each person's self-world relation. The prototype of the passive pole would be rooted in breast-sucking implied, for instance, by WoGaye's soul that supposedly prefers the cadaverous *ingaalye* fluids and putrefied flesh of corpses rather than the flesh of living humans = pigs. The active pole is on display in the motely imagery of manifest killing and eating. The form of ultra-aggressivity, such as evident in OMitane's womba showings, may be interpreted as a manifestation of his own aggression turned against himself, echoing the original experiences of

As we talked about these developments within his soul, there were moments when OAp laughed and spat in revulsion while telling me about the cutting and eating of men's throats, commenting that this was all really "bad" (*kuluwye*). He emphasized, as he always did, that he talked out about his dream-showings to other fellow villagers and some shamans, for if he did not, he would become a true womba. They all told him that these were really bad showings. He knew, however, due to his shamanistic dream-showings that he had an exceptionally strong soul. A subsiding of these shamanistic showings in very recent years, however, gave him reason for concern. OAp was adamant that this was happening because of some shaman (*aamnye napalye iye*) envious of his soul powers and his prospect of becoming a powerful shaman. OAp's powers portended that he would be able to outdo the local shamans and thereby become rich. To prevent this, OAp argued, some local envious shaman was trying to block out his soul, which in turn deprived him of these empowering visionary experiences. But as it happened, in February 1994, he fell asleep in the middle of the day and had a most potent shamanic dream, which occasioned another discussion of his soul powers, their blocking and, as this dream-showing clearly indicated, the prospect that these might become freed again. In his view, the blocking is done by means of an appropriate *ququna yakale* (word-voicing = spell) that is spoken over some food, betel nut, or tobacco and given to the unsuspecting person who consumes it. This sort of action is the work of *ki'nye*, which indeed might be glossed as "sorcery." In OAp's self-understanding, this

---

his conjunction with victims whom he killed via close bodily contact by means of mostly a club and axe. Following such a kill he, as every other warrior-killer, had to undergo a purification rite that divested him of the blood and brain-substance (the desired target was the shattering of the head) of his victims.

kind of action must have depotentiated his soul so that his shamanic visions, caused by the wild forest spirits (*hyaqaye ilymane*), have left him, at least for a while. If there was a moment when OAp emphasized the truly malignant powers and activities that in his view characterize the Yagwoia people as a whole, it was exactly this nefarious *ki'nye* craftiness motivated by envy and greediness for other people's soul-powers and possessions.

In the spectrum of life^death powers that drive and sustain the Yagwoia lifeworld, neither OAp's self-evaluation nor the views of any other Yagwoia suggested that the womba condition of a person's soul would have a radically negative valency. This is symptomatic of the overall character of the Yagwoia moral sense of self, its sensibilities, and the dynamics of culpability. If judged in terms of the above facts, which reveal a great deal more about Yagwoia moral substance than any explicit pronouncement that any of them might make, one may say that womba is not an "evil" capacity of the soul but an extreme development of the appetitive passion of the soul pivoting on its generative oral nucleus. It clearly relates to *Eating*, the nuclear oral-cannibalistic constellation of matrifiliation at the core of the Yagwoia kinship self and its life^death circuitry. The correlative patrifilial loop is the mirror image, wherein specifically the F > S link, determined as *Planting*, is a one-way incorporation of the father's bone by the son, marked by a mode of pre-oedipal dynamics (Mimica 1991, 2007b, 2010b). This matrixial cannibalistic determination of Yagwoia kinship selfhood (microcosmos) may well be taken as a conditioning factor as to why the womba affliction of the soul bears a nonlethal coefficient of culpability so that no Yagwoia womba-person risks a violent termination or expulsion from the body social.[12] The ouroboric dynamics is such that

---

12. However, given the current evangelical climate promoted by a PNG state-church partnership, this may change.

it can and does metabolize all modalities of its substance. Whether "raw," "rotten," "putrid," or "cooked," they are all palatable, digestible and, therefore, nourishing of the ouroboric whole, which ceaselessly totalizes itself qua all its parts (Mimica 1991).

CHAPTER 4

The spectrum of Yagwoia cannibalism

The ouroboric dynamics of the Yagwoia body social—
their collective (un)conscious and the cultural imaginary
as a whole—require an amplification in reference to the
overall configuration of their cannibalistic practices, past
and present, and the correlative moral (ethos) and hedonic
sensibilities. The presentation so far shows that in the
womba mode of cannibalistic desire one's soul craves for
and eats meat (pork = human flesh) in any condition: raw,
cooked, putrid. In other words, the craving extends to the full
metamorphic spectrum that bodily substance, understood
as the immanent incarnated life-flow (libido^mortido),
undergoes in its ceaseless movement, from gestation in the
womb (via implantation = coitus) to the decomposition of
the corpse before and after the disposal, which traditionally
was the object of mortuary necrophagy. And, as we saw, the
womba desire, apart from raw flesh, cathects in particular
the putrid substance of corpses. Here I want to emphasize
that this is so regardless of whether a person has had
an experience of actual necrophagy. OAp, for instance,
never experienced this, but his oneiric experiences show
otherwise. Yet, considering his overall socialization and the
development of his libido^mortido, while different from the
life experience of his father OMitane and so many other men
and women among whom OAp grew up, his (un)conscious

has been informed and shaped by the common matrix of their distinctively Yagwoia cultural imaginary. This points to its radical intersubjective reality and objectivity. This chapter examines this off-putting yet most symptomatic expression of the intersubjective transmission and palpable reality of the womba complex.

An inside perspective

When I first inquired about cannibalism, the Iqwaye denied having ever practiced it but at the same time imputed it to their non-Yagwoia-speaking neighbors. Both the exo- and the endo-versions were a sensitive subject to probe in the early phase of my first fieldwork. Later on this mood changed; in fact, some of the most revealing expressions of the practice were made quite spontaneously.[1] The most

---

1. A word for those readers interested in the kind of issues that gave rise to the well-known anthropological controversies on cannibalism (e.g., Arens 1979; Obeyesekere 2005; Goldman 1999; Gillison 2007), including such a case as Marano's (1985) critique of the *windigo* psychosis as a "culture-bound syndrome." For my purpose here, I have no good enough reason to engage with these discourses. The chief problem with them is the absence of (preferably psychoanalytic) self-reflection of one's (un)conscious, moral sensibilities, defenses, and correlative biases that underpin especially those arguments that frame cannibalism primarily as the projection of White observers. Without such reflection one is open to motley idealizations (easily turning sanctimonious) and correlative false consciousness. From my perspective, imagination and phantasy figure as a constitutive dimension of all cultural forms, not just of cannibalism. I take the cannibalistic desire to be a basic modality of the oral drive overwhelmingly shaped by the dynamics of maternal envelopment. This primordial intersubjective matrix produces a range of phantasy projections and, as such, gives rise to cultural practices and value systems in a myriad of concrete

memorable one relevant to the present discussion occurred in the context of pork consumption. On one occasion I had in my hut a group of men, OMitane among them, all close friends, whom I had invited to eat a large piece of pork. I used to do this every so often for their delight. I would eat one or two pieces or abstain altogether, rather disliking pork. As the men were munching big chunks with utmost relish, OMitane remarked that I was behaving as a truly good (exemplary) Iqwaye father would, abstaining from eating for the benefit of his children and not expecting to be reciprocated, thus acting in willing self-denial.[2] Then, after a momentary pause, all the while still eating, he went on to relate how once, at the time of fighting (thus before the arrival of Australian kiaps [district officers), a fighting group of Iwolaqa Malyce (a neighboring Yagwoia group) went looking for game (i.e., human prey) among Baruya speakers in the Ucelapiye area and, having killed a few including a woman, returned to their home area where they carved and ate them at a *hiqwona* (bachelors hut). One man, HM, who did not go on the raid, came in and, assuming that they were eating pork, asked for some leftovers. They pointed to one

---

positive forms and sublimations, as well as inhibitions and prohibitions. As far as the Yagwoia and their immediate neighbors, the Pataye, are concerned, I have no doubts about the factual character of their exo- and endo-cannibalistic practices (e.g., Mimica 2006: 45–46). There are also accounts in the literature, especially on Melanesia, by anthropologists who witnessed cannibalism (e.g., Poole 1983). Also, Koch's (1970a, 1970b) papers contain matter-of-fact accounts and descriptions by his Jale informants that are anything but primarily their (or the ethnographer's) projections. For the mode of endo-practice that deeply resonates with the Yagwoia practice, see the classic paper by Gillison (1983).

2. This framing as father was most unusual since his entire lineage generally regarded me as a "sister's son," thus that they were my "mothers" and that I was irreversibly indebted to them for my bodily life (flesh).

piece that was left in the ashes. Without paying attention he grabbed it, shook off the ash, and plunged his teeth into it. He had pretty much gulped down the lot when they informed him that this had not been pork but the vagina of the woman they had killed, which is why nobody wanted to eat it, even though it was cooked. From that day onwards he was known as *Quleqwany-onya* (the one who ate vagina-third born). The account provoked a rapturous laughter that, no doubt, echoed the original situation.[3] What is symptomatic here is that OMitane, who had a distinguished fighting career, was motivated to narrate this story precisely in the context of a particularly pleasant experience of pork eating, a genuine free gift that entailed no obligation to give back or repay. Furthermore, it was a perfect expression of the libidio^mortido ambivalence that dominates Yagwoia orality and underpins their gustatory sensibilities pertaining to pork and game, as well as the identification of woman and pig.

Three other so-to-speak "axiological" images have to be explicated. One is the Yagwoia idea of a "good father." The

---

3. All Yagwoia nicknames are predicated on some genuine happening or concrete attributes that came to affect and/or redefine the bearer's identity and that the person lives with willy-nilly. With this event, HM's nickname entered the genealogical memory. When OMitana recounted the story, one of his classificatory ZSs asked whether this had truly happened. Without hesitation OMitane said that the enquirer could ask a descendant of this ancestor who would surely confirm it. Some years later, an Iwolaqa-Malyace man confirmed the event had taken place as described, but corrected one point: HM's descendant was not the man OMitana had named to his classificatory ZS, a shaman and renowned *aapiyice* (singer) whom I happened to know well, but someone else. For my part, regardless of the story's phantasy-coefficient, I am convinced the account was factual precisely because the event was codified in the nickname affixed to HM's birth-order suffix, "third-born."

destiny of the father's "bone," that is, his libidinal power, is to be irreversibly incorporated specifically by his son(s). This is principally expressed in the view and practice that one does not have to give back anything to one's father while a father should willingly give everything of his and of himself to his son(s) in order to maximally implant himself into his issue (*uwye*), thus ensuring his continuity. The father > child (son) relation is that of Planting, in contrast to the M/ MB < ZCh one, which is that of Eating. In that regard, no Yagwoia would profess to eat pork (or any other edible) in the presence of his/her mothers, and definitely not in the presence of one's (male) mother's breast; instead, one ought to surrender to him the whole lot. This vital ouroboric circuity of kinship, generative of the bodily person, can be usefully schematized as a Möbius strip or a Klein bottle. The inner dimension is that of the paternal semen/bone flow irreversibly going from F > Ch/S (patri-filiation) while the outer dimension of the maternal "flesh," itself derived from the mother's blood and milk, is eaten back by the Mothers qua the substance of life-payments. The dynamics of the father's bone Planting (self-implantation) is a mirror image of the mothers' Eating (reincorporation), the two circuits established through the sexual conjunction between one's father's penis and one mother's vagina-womb, wherein in utero one comes into being and, postpartum, eats—and is eaten/planted—from the net-bag to the final decomposition (eating) into the world-body, via the mouths = stomachs of the mothers.[4]

---

4. See Mimica (1991) for the topological implications of the dynamics of ouroboric kinship selfhood. It is significant that, in the wake of Yagwoia incorporation into the capitalist world system, the Tok Pisin metaphor for the matrifilial "meat [*namdje*]/flesh" identity of one's sister's child is "profit" (sometimes also "bank"): for example, "Em profit bilong mipela" or, in the vernacular, "*Nengwolye* profit."

The second image is that of the human prey as game (marsupials). "Hunting opossum" is an image of raiding as well as of the treatment of novices, especially in the first two initiations (the first of which includes nose-piercing and insemination) and undergoing further transformations in the remaining three. The primary context, however, is that of the "childbirth marsupial" hunted by the neonate's father (see ch. 3). All of these variants are predicated on the cosmogonic birth > death > rebirth of the first neonate = marsupial *Wuiy-Malyoqwa*, through collective (fraternal) insemination of a genital-less man who for that reason became the first woman (see Mimica 1981, 1991). The vernacular category *hiye* designates all game (marsupials and the water rat) and as such can be glossed both as "marsupial" and "game." In Tok Pisin, it is rendered as both *kapul* (commonly rendered in English as "opossum") and *abus* (meat). However, the latter is commonly intended as "marsupial meat" or "game." When the reference is to the intertribal raids and fighting, this is frequently rendered as "wokim abus long ol" ("doing game/meat on" a certain group). Whenever a person was killed, the killer(s) would bark like dogs, signaling that the "prey" was caught; the same voicing was done upon return to the village. However, it is only the Iqwaye-Yagwoia territorial group and the eponymous Iqwaye *latice* group that have the distinction of being *wokiye* (dogs). The Iqwaye *latice* alone owns the cosmogonic dog-identity of the primal child-marsupial man, at once hunter and prey.[5]

---

5. *Wuiy-Malyoqwa* is a syzygy mythologem: he is both dog and harpy-eagle (*pace*), expressing both the terrestrial and the solar-celestial self-twined "hunter" identity while the *hiye* (marsupial), as an arboreal animal, connects the two poles and thus stands for both the ouroboric cosmic tree (self-contained phallic world-womb = axis mundi) and the sun^moon who cosmogonically ascended into the sky as a marsupial shot by Imacoqwa who in turn is the autogenic cosmic androgyne and the world-body (see Mimica 1981, 1988, 1991).

The third value implicit in OMitane's account concerns the woman = pig identification. Its most explicit articulation is in the fifth initiation ceremony. This is the context in which verbal instructions (*ququ-teqace*, literally "word/talk of counsel") reach their utmost climax. They pertain to the Yagwoia ethos and life values, especially the relation between shell-generation (*ungye*, representing wealth) and children through whom man's "bone" (his solar-libidinal power = "spirit") is perpetuated in the mediation of pig and woman. As they face a ritual edifice whose focal display expresses the seminal-generative effluence of shells (they also subsume money) from the woman's vagina (symbolized by a double pig-tusk necklace), the novices are subjected to instructions by fully initiated men who, most importantly, have sired children. The emotional quality of their counsel oscillates between a didactic expostulation, harangue, and, depending on the phase of the unfolding ritual action, outright mockery and jeering intended to deliver the last salve of humiliation. One of the fundamental statements made is that the novices should not think that shells (wealth) and everything else they bring about (principally one's woman and, through her, his children) come from simply anywhere. They come from pigs and one should know that every man's first wife is a pig because this one alone gives him the shells that will allow him to get the other woman, the one with whom he will copulate and make children and replace himself qua his bone. All this derives from that first "pig-woman."

At the same time, every man is aware of the fact that the "first woman" is pigs raised principally by his mother, though with some contributions by his father. Moreover, in addition to the shells that the "pig-wife" brought about due to his mother's hard work, it is also the "floodwater" (i.e., shells) obtained as his sister's bride-price,[6] which joined the

---

6. The "flood water" (*aalye wa:le*) image condenses both the fact that in his sister's body another man implanted himself qua

ones obtained through his mother's pigs, that have procured him the other wife through whose womb he has now fully consummated his manhood as the solar source of life.

The sexual aspect of the pig-woman-wealth nexus is fully articulated in both the ritual and everyday spheres of life. To the extent that pig is a total libidinal object (as is wealth) that, in its core, is invested with the primal object of desire, the mother,[7] there is only one known instance of its so-to-speak de-sublimation and de-symbolization, that is, its translation into a literal act of pleasure consummation. In the early 2000s in the Hyaqwang-Ilyce territorial group, a man was caught in flagrante copulating with a pig that (and this made the case ever more outrageous) was not his, so that the offence also included theft. The outraged owner took the offender to the police court in Menyamya where he was severely roughed up and ordered to pay a hefty compensation to the pig's owner. Being sullied, the animal was deemed inedible and no longer of a state that it could be further circulated within the body social. Such circulation entails the libidinal flow qua pigs and things to undergo its maximal generative transformation, which makes every mode of substance properly edible. A further element of this veritable dialectical "turning into the opposite" (and "transvaluation" of if not all values then

---

his bone and thus opened her up when she gave birth; this birth-water delivers a child to his ZH for which the latter paid the bride-price shells. Retrospectively, then, that is the reason for their identification as the "flood water" by virtue of which man has become the true mother's breast. Prospectively, in the context of the fifth initiation, his situation is exactly the same as his ZH's in relation to himself. The initiate has sired his first child, hence released his wife's "flood water" thanks to the shells that come from his first, pig-wife (thus embodying irreducibly man's maternal—flesh identity) and his WB is now his (initiate's) child's bona fide mother's breast.

7. Accordingly, the full nexus is mother/breast (object-of-desire) = pig = woman = wealth.

certainly a fundamental one) was that the offender was also a member of the Christian Rivival (*Rivaivelist*) group whose leaders were trying hard to win new members in a context where many did not like these newcomers intruding on the established Lutheran and SDA congregations. Thus, some Yagwoia used this opportunity to rail against these *Rivaivelists*, pointing out that the pig-molester exemplifies the kind of aberrant creed they promote.

Exo- and endo- modes

The Yagwoia exo-cannibalistic mode applied to those people who spoke languages different from the Yagwoia. When it comes to the logic of exo^endo dimensionality, which articulates the Yagwoia social body, then it should be emphasized that the difference in language, whose medium is the orally produced human speech-sound, defines the closure of the social body in respect of its affinal circuity. The ideal was that one ought not to marry (and thus copulate with) those who speak a different language because this is most likely to ruin the name combinations of the male progeny resulting from such unions (see Mimica 1991). Therefore, the social body ought to be kept homo-lingually endogamous, closed in on itself. But the counterpoint to this restriction was that once you copulate, the names (i.e., the speech substance) become mutually compatible. And indeed, despite the prevalence of intra-territorial and homo-lingual endogamy, the Yagwoia, nonetheless, did and do marry their hetero-lingual neighbors, this being principally the case between the Iqwaye-Yagwoia and the Menya-speaking Pataye with whom they formed a military alliance early in the twentieth century. It dissolved at the onset of the twenty-first century, the process to which I observed in various phases of intensification over the last thirty years.

A downside of this alliance was that they were principally fighting other Yagwoia-speaking groups, which negatively impacted on the Iqwaye as it inhibited them from consuming their slain homo-lingual fellow-Yagwoia. For the Paṭaye, in contrast, the killed men and women were their proper *hiye* (marsupials), which has the generic sense of "game-meat" (by contrast to pork-meat). However, I was told that some Iqwaye felt quite uninhibited in the company of their Menya-speaking allies, leading them not only to kill their homo-lingual NgWa:ce neighbors but also to eat them. The "mixed company," as it were, enabled these Iqwaye men to suspend their inhibitions and blot out the fact that they were, in effect, acting not just homo-phagously but virtually autophagously.[8]

As is commonly the case, among the Yagwoia too necrophagy was an endo-cannibalistic practice. In terms of its ouroboric structural significance, it was a major mode of the consummation of the internal self-closure of the social body and its life^death self-circuity. This was specifically articulated in the domain of cross-sex siblingship (B^Z), which is also constituted through the process of *Eating*. I will give a bare outline of the practice. The significance of cross-sex siblingship was most acutely expressed in one specific context of mortuary practices, namely the smoking of the corpse and the consumption of putrid fluids emanating from the corpse. This practice no longer exists due to its suppression by the Australian colonial government, virtually from its first arrival in the Menyamya area in the early 1950s. Among the Iqwaye, corpse smoking and related practices persisted until the mid-1960s when they were irrevocably abandoned. It is significant that the Australian Lutheran missionaries took a quite neutral position toward this practice on the pretext that there was nothing in the Bible that would stipulate and/or justify its prohibition (Menyamya Patrol Report 1963). As for

---

8. For these and related aspects of exo^endo dynamics in the structuration of the Yagwoia social body and the life^death (libidinal^mortidinal) self-circuity of sociality, see Mimica (1991).

its origin, the Iqwaye see it as not being their indigenous *hyiuwye* (custom) but as an import into Yagwoia groups from hetero-lingual foreigners (*ulyce*) such as the Nakocuwiye (Kapau speakers); the mediators in this transmission were the Menya-speaking groups.

Although corpse smoking no longer exists, the prolonged handling of corpses has remained quite intact in the current situation (throughout my research spanning from 1977 to 2010). As such the presence of death in the form of the spectacle of a corpse's germinative decomposition in the midst and zest of quotidian life has lost very little of its former intensity and splendor, a veritable celebration of the Yagwoia way of ouroboric being-in-the-world. The consumption of the cadaverous fluids (*ingaalye*) was as follows. During the smoking of a corpse, copious fluids would drip from its pores and orifices, especially from the mouth. The corpse was attended to by female relatives and, if the deceased was a man, by his sister. Among other activities the sister would immerse bunches of *kunyile*, a green leafy vegetable (*Oenanthe javanica*), in the gelatinous fluids until they became thoroughly saturated. These were then rolled and inserted into a bamboo tube and cooked in the fire. Once steamed, the vegetables were eaten by the deceased's sister, her small children, as well as other *female* relatives and their small children. I emphasize that this was practiced *only* by women and small children. According to informants no man would avail himself of this morsel.[9]

Experience of necrophagy

Now let me relate this summary description to a concrete experience. I will invoke Qang again who shared with me

---

9. For a fuller treatment of Yagwoia practices, see Mimica (1991, 2008c). For a comparison, see Dupeyrat (1954: 220–24) and Gillison (1983, 1993).

a memorable childhood experience. Once, when he was a little boy, his mother went to the garden, leaving him in the care of a big and strong woman. Qang said that this woman would lift him up with just one arm, as if he were feather-light, and place him on the top of net-bags that were hanging from her forehead and hung down her back. They were inside her house and he was crying because his mother was gone and the woman placated him by pointing to the roof-rafters and telling him to look up—there were two marsupials for them to eat. These were the corpses of two men, father and son, hanging in two net-bags over the fire-hearth and getting smoked. Both had been killed by the Iqwaye. She told him not to cry but to go to fetch the *kunyile* vegetables so they could scoop up the fluids that were dripping from the corpses. When we talked about these now abandoned components of the mortuary practices, Qang would often recall this particular childhood experience. He said that he was somewhat perplexed when she told him that those two were "our meat."

This is a telling example of a tacit yet discursive articulation of the goodness of not just human flesh (displaced to marsupials) but of bodily dissolution pitched in the alimentary-gustatory register. The big woman told him not to cry (because of his mother's absence) for there was a tasty "game-meat" for him (and her) to eat and that this would fill in his mother's absence. The promise of a filled stomach is intended to transmute the absence of the primal, maternal self-object into a palatable and pleasurable substitute that atones the momentary anxiety. This substitutive and atoning use of food is a universal human predilection. Food commonly compensates for this sort of separation experience and for other modes of self-privative anxiety, frustration, and self-dissatisfaction. Through eating a distressed child makes up for the absence or the deficiency of the maternal container and the contentment it provides, aiming thus to regain the primal dual-unity of the container and the contained. In the ouroboric lifeworld of the Yagwoia, however, the maternal-domestic contexture of the food and womb as well as of the tomb, thus the real dissolving human cadaver destined for the actual alimentary incorporation, has been actualized in acute form.[10]

This memory from Qang's childhood is illuminating and points to deeper significances of the Yagwoia necrophagy and cannibalistic (both exo^endo) nexus as a total phenomenon. The womba complex appears as one particular—negative—modality of this larger dynamic of cannibalistic striving. The womba complex has to be contemplated in this context precisely because its primary reality is that of the desire and passions of the soul and its objectifications as oneiric and wakeful hallucinatory spectacles of ambivalent suffering. Irrespective of the fact that as a young man Qang was plagued by malignant womba showings (to which he never succumbed), his childhood memory of necrophagy had tangential links to them. This connection leads to another trajectory of the Yagwoia cannibalistic complex (now seen as a total phenomenon), namely the desire for being eaten by the mother and reincorporated into her womb, albeit articulated as a tacit phantasy of blissful self-dissolution (Mimica 2008c).[11] The prospect of self-dissolution and

---

10. Parenthetically, a professional mortician and embalmer who also studied anthropology once attended a lecture I gave on Yagwoia mortuary practices and told me how he could relate to this. According to him it is a common experience among his professional colleagues to develop an enormous appetite while working on a corpse.

11. In 2008, while in Goroka, I had a conversation with a Fore man who used to work in the local hospital. He told me that he read what some anthropologists wrote about the necrophagy practiced by his people. His passionate objection to these accounts was that they missed the fundamental aspect, namely love. He said: "You [White people] do not know what true love is. There is no truer love than the one shown by your sister who wants to eat you." In this regard, see the Yagwoia view of the normative sister's passions in relation

absorption into the maternal container may induce the feeling of a deep self-contentment and blissful self-extinction into primal germinative liquidity. The cadaverous corpse manifests this potently, not just as a visual spectacle but, especially, in its stench that spreads densely and widely and whose quiddity is inhaled. In that olfactory mode the corpse is literally eaten in massive amounts by all those who participate in mortuary séances.

Taste and smell are potently cross-modal, on par with sight and hearing (sound), so that smell readily translates into taste and vice versa. It can be rightly said that the nose stimulates the mouth (palate) and refers it to the source of smell as the object of taste and, reciprocally, the mouth acts upon the nose. But the two are by no means mutually confirming. Thus, in the case of Yagwoia necrophagy, when an Iqwaye woman of yore was asked by a (classificatory) grandson what the steamed putrid *ingaalye* fluids tasted like, she replied: "To you the smell is off-putting but when eaten it tastes like salt!," thus indicating that it is indeed palatable and therefore covetous. The inhalation of stench is the actual mode through which the necrophagous experience continues without corpse fluids being eaten: "I am full of the *amnye piye* [literally stink-person = corpse]" is not an uncommon declaration when, during mortuary séances, a mourner comes out of the hut to get some less saturated—fresher—air.[12]

---

to her comportment to her dead brother's body (Mimica 1991).

12. Yagwoia necrophagy had a coefficient of duress but not to the exclusion of a degree of ambivalent pleasure both in the smell and taste, as the old lady's remark states candidly (see also Qang's childhood reminiscence). Furthermore, the vegetables were steam cooked, and this would certainly have made some difference. Human passions of death, as of sex and love, can put up with and overcome all sorts of duress. On balance, although pungent and off-putting, this was a relatively mild practice

The intensity of the smell of decomposing corpses varies but is subject to a patterned transformation. In the incipient phase the smell is often aromatic, especially

---

when compared with, say, finger-lopping, practiced in various parts of New Guinea but extremely uncommon among the Yagwoia. There was only one case in recent times (2002) by a man. He did this when his ZS, a very young man, committed suicide by hanging. But the MB's motivation was questioned by the dead man's father. The father thought his son's MB resorted to finger-lopping in order to demand a higher death payment, in terms of loss of his (sister's) child + finger = heightened self-loss. To be sure, although this framing was motivated by the father's passionate self-concern—he himself was undergoing the double self-loss (son + pending death-payment)—it does not negate the mother's breast's passions for his lost child. Indeed, the male mother, qua his self-inflicted loss, wants his ZS's body maximally back—in the form of a highest payment he can extract.

The most intense expression of grief among the Yagwoia takes the following common forms listed in terms of their perceived intensity scale: laceration/cutting of the forehead with a knife and/or a rock (men and women); smashing of shell valuables, burning of banknotes, and burning down one's own house. The latter three, characteristically male outpours, also occur in contexts when a person feels unjustly wronged and is thus compelled to turn in on himself. The extreme is suicide, common among both men and women. A person may also commit suicide if they suffer from unbearable pain and/or debilitating sickness.

Regarding the practice of finger-lopping in PNG, many years ago the late Marvyn Meggitt reported in a departmental seminar at the Australian National University that Mae Enga indentured laborers would offer to lop off a finger or two—for a fee—to anyone whose relation has died and, therefore, might wish to avail themselves of this Enga funeral custom even though that person might not be an Enga. In short, when it comes to the passions of the human soul and spirit, duress may not be an issue at all.

when one is some distance from its source, say outside the homestead and the hut containing the corpse. The closer one gets, the more the smell has an impact on the palate: one simultaneously smell-tastes its ambiguous quality—at once attractive and repulsive. After two or three days, the smell becomes a thick and heavy stench that saturates everything. The following description of my very first experience of mortuary practices (October 1977) will suffice. As I was walking to the place where T-M's body had been brought, a light but steady flow of wind was blowing through the upper Yalqwoyi valley. At first the breeze appeared mildly aromatic, then it turned into an odor that smell-tasted like a blend of over-fermented peaches and some unidentified agglomeration of rotten fruits. For a moment I thought that something like this must be the source for this odd mixture of smell and pleasant fragrance. As I proceeded, the breeze became sweeter yet carried a tinge of sickening pungency. The ambiguous quality got stronger the closer I neared the bend in the path. As I then came around the corner and saw the place, I realized the source of this sickeningly sweet stench: surrounded by young women and children, there was T-M's body, covered with a bluish linen and surrounded by a few bunches of semi-dried *tekiye* reeds to produce a bit of shade from the sun's heat.

This smell is not that of "death" but a manifestation of at once the libidinal signature of the deceased person's embodiment and his/her alimentary cum sexual life-history (Mimica 2003a). It is also the cosmo-ontological mirror image of the intrauterine gestation: the germinative metamorphosis of the bodily substance whose luno-solar (microcosmic) life-substance (soul) is undergoing liquefaction and dis-incarnation whereby the flesh becomes absorbed into the ouroboric world-body, the macrocosmic container of all that there is, was, and ever will be. The mortuary dirges accompanying this process articulate the macrocosmic aspect of decomposition in a most poignant mode of, one can say, Yagwoia onto-poetic self-expression (Mimica 2003a, 2008c).[13]

The prolonged company of bloating corpses, the inhalation of stench, the practice of bodily contact and smearing, especially of young nubile women and children,[14] with corpse fluids, and the intersubjective (group) dynamics of mortuary séances and their onto-poetic aesthesis define the Yagwoia sociality of death and dying in which I participated on numerous occasions and experienced in the depths of my (un)conscious. The mortuary practices intensify the ordinarily more tacit and diffuse cannibalistic dynamics that permeate the Yagwoia lifeworld. They make more palpable its generative archetypal matrix, the ouroboric imaginary. I will illustrate its intersubjective reality in the way it was actualized in my (un)conscious, that is, someone who was not born and socialized in the Yagwoia lifeworld but was opened up to and affected by it. I will briefly discuss one of my dreams whose manifest content bears acute witness to specifically the intimate bond between the stench-mediated necrophagy and the womba complex. It occurred during my first fieldwork (1977–79) when I was immersed in the Yagwoia lifeworld for over two years.

Briefly, in the dream-space I saw a putrefied human hand while a voice emanating from a dark void was instructing

---

13. It is significant that the Yagwoia men of knowledge regard mortuary and healing dirges/songs as merely the creations of ordinary human beings. By contrast, the *Qwolamnye Aapiye*, a veritable cosmogonic song performed at the onset of the first initiation ceremony, is unequivocally affirmed as Imacoqwa's (ouroboric cosmic androgyne) creation. Every aspect of this song, especially its syntactically articulated poetic form, supports that view.

14. This is especially the case when the deceased (male or female) was a person (his/her soul) possessed of some distinctive ability (strength), as, for example, a warrior, someone skilled in attracting wealth, a planter, a hard-working gardener, or someone who excelled in raising pigs.

me, "Eat it! It is pig." The voice kept on repeating these words and trying to push the hand into my mouth; but no human figure was discernible. Although the voice was very convincing in its insistence that the hand was a piece of pork, what stopped me from biting into it was the overwhelming stench of a cadaver. The voice persisted, pushing the hand at me, but eventually I repelled the hand from my face and screamed, "No—it is a human hand!" As I did so, I woke up, retaining a fervent sense of the stench that, although intra-psychic, I felt as an outside presence saturating the air around me. Only after a minute or so the sense tailed off and the stench evaporated. There was no recent mortuary séance that could have been the immediate stimulus of the dream. When I told OT, one of my coworkers, about the dream the next morning, he as a matter of course said that this was a womba trying to dupe me. Just as well, he commented, that I did not plunge my teeth into the "pork," thanks to what he called my strong soul that made me resist the goading voice and repel so strongly the putrid morsel.

I should say that since my earliest childhood I have been a lucid dreamer. What amazed me about this dream, however, was the dissonance I experienced (while dreaming) between the visual content (a putrid hand), the persistent and convincing lingual-sonic deception (the voice saying that it was pig, hence perfectly edible), and the intensifying stench that overwhelmed the dream-scene. It was this last sensory quality, an expression of the emotional welling up of my resistance, which overrode the persuasive power of the voice (my archaic, maternal super-ego) and decisively jolted me to reject this intra-psychic commanding presence. It can be said that the insistent voice and the intensifying stench were a dynamic mirror-splitting of a single ambivalent circuit of the orally calibrated desire for incorporation; hence the simultaneous presence of attraction and repulsion. The latter won.

This completes my survey of the inner relations between the womba complex and the wider domain of Yagwoia cannibalism. In order to further problematize the issue of Yagwoia moral substance, I now turn to say a few words about Yagwoia *ki'nye*—sorcery—to show how it differs from the womba complex and to probe more deeply into the problematic of moral sensibilities within the matrix of their ouroboric lifeworld.

CHAPTER 5

On *ki'nye* (sorcery) and the mother's breast's malediction

The most important dimension of *ki'nye* activity is the cosmo-ontological significance of the speech-word (*ququne*).[1] This is so because, regardless of its material implements, substances, and gestural performance, there is no *ki'nye* without the use of an appropriate *ququne yakale* (spell). One learns them from one's father, mother, mother's brother, grandparents; one can also purchase them or simply pay a person who knows a spell for the appropriate purpose to perform it. As verbal productions, however, spells are not conscious creations by an ego but a boon bestowed by spirits upon living mortals, either in dreams or in possession states. Only by means of such received *ququne yakale* in which constructive or destructive power is immanent—that is, the life^death powers inherent in the macrocosmos at large—can one practice *ki'nye*.[2] Thus, although *ki'nye* is a self-consciously volitional activity, the root-source of its power, as of all spell-dependent activities, is external to the mortal human practitioners. One may passionately desire to use *ki'nye* but unless one has the right instrument, that

---

1. *Ququne* can also be glossed as "speech," "utterance," or "words."
2. On the Yagwoia view of speech, see Mimica (2014a).

is, the right kind of spell, or has someone with that kind of knowledge to act on one's behalf, the soul's desire remains impotent.

There is a spectrum of *ki'nye* and its application. For instance, there are common *ki'nye* applications that everybody uses, such as those that protect one's gardens and betel palm groves from an illegitimate user who might be tempted to pick nuts without permission. The *ki'nye* spell that protects betel nuts targets teeth so that the person who chews the be-spelled nuts will suffer the loss of all teeth. Central in this category of spells is the invocation of the frog because this animal has no teeth, which is the desired effect of the spell. Although the loss of teeth is by no means a negligible matter, this kind of *ki'nye*-induced harm is a self-validating use of destructive powers: one acts with the intention of inflicting grievous bodily harm in order oneself not to get harmed, albeit in a different register—dispossession of a valuable cultivar.

This example illustrates the lower end of the spectrum of *ki'nye* lethality and one can go on listing examples that will plot its escalating trajectory, climaxing in the complete physical destruction of the targeted person and things. Although it exemplifies the purposeful operation of destructive desire and volition within the social body, to get a proper perspective on the centrality of the malignant—mortally destructive—powers and the will to apply them, constitutive of Yagwoia kinship intersubjectivity, I have to say a few words about, so to speak, the kernel of kernels of the life^death dynamics. This is the power that the "mother's breast" (maternal uncle, MB) has over his sister's children effected in the enactment of that special *ququna yakale* that can be rendered as a "mother's breast's lethal malediction" (curse). I gloss it so because not every Yagwoia, especially men, would readily see this spell application as an act of *ki'nye*, despite the fact that there is seemingly no overt distinction between them. What difference there is between them is shown below.

The mirror-circuit of the mother's breast's malediction

The will to destruction and concomitant murderousness reign supreme within the cosmo-ontological determinants of the Yagwoia lifeworld and its cultural imaginary. The intensity of numerous acts of physical violence in Yagwoia sociality are an authentic expression of the ouroboric life^death dynamics that drive Yagwoia existence as a whole and, especially, their kinship sociality, which in turn illuminates certain universal aspects of this regal domain of anthropological inquiry, recently ontologically characterized by Sahlins (2011, 2013) as the "mutuality of being." Just to notice in passing, unless one specifies the contents of what "mutuality" subsumes, this phrasing is likely to induce a projection of rapturous qualities upon the facticity of kinship sociality. Yet it would be mistaken to think of the ouroboric dynamics of selfhood within the Yagwoia field of relatedness as if it were driven by a polarization into such seemingly clear-cut values as good and evil. Here, human selfhood incorporates no Kantian "categorical moral imperative" whose long historical genesis, in the wake of the Axial Age, was mediated by the Socratic philosophical framing of the self and soul as well as by the relation with such a Judeo-Christian archetypal pair as the All-Good God and the Devil, a personification of Radical Evil; nor a "categorical imperative" that became coterminous, in the wake of modernity and the Enlightenment, with the landmark feature of Western egoity—the power of self-positing, that is, the pursuit of human auto-nomy over and against divine hetero-nomy. Accordingly, Sahlins' rhapsodic "mutuality of being" (like Fortes' [1969] formal-legalistic "axiom of kinship amity") has to be substantiated in concrete terms: among the Yagwoia, their ouroboric "relationality" is nothing less than incorporative-devouring dynamics of Planting and Eating (Mimica 1991).[3]

---

3. This, of course, does not square well with M. Strathern's (1988) influential discourses on Melanesian dividuals. One gets the

In this perspective, the existential reality of ouroboric good and bad (rather than Evil) is sustained by a different cosmo-ontological matrix. Here all values derive from the fundamental self-value of one and the same auto-generative (self-eating = self-copulating) androgynous Cosmic Phallus that is also the ouroboric Cosmic Tree of Life^Death. Its dynamics is that of auto-polarization, that is, simultaneous self-disjunction and conjunction. In the domain of kinship relatedness this translates into a network of any self's fluctuating cline of relative differentiation between *self-sameness* and *self-difference*, or in somewhat less familiar terms, me and the mirror-not-me. Note that I am not speaking here of Self and Other since Other(ness) among the Yagwoia is the product of the self-differentiation of the Self. This is so because in the ouroboric lifeworld all difference, starting with sexuation and sexed embodiment, is generated through the self-splitting of the primordial phallic self-same bi-unity of the Cosmic Self, the ONE that is ALL. Accordingly, just as femaleness is the self-difference within the phallic ONE that is the bi-unity of fe^maleness, so is otherness a mirror-self-difference of self-generating self-sameness. In other words, all polarities exist solely on the condition of the simultaneous conjunction and disjunction (^) of their terms. Any X is what it is qua its mirror self-same-difference ^X (Mimica 1991).

This dialectic logic underpins the narcissistic dynamics of talionic intentionality at work in Yagwoia intersubjectivity, but its crystalline institutional expression is the mother's breast malediction (curse)—the act of willful destruction

---

impression that the ethnographers who accept this image of human personhood give little thought to what concretely the psychic reality of dividuality and its intersubjective field is. One ought to pay attention to the drives and desires sustaining this immanent divisiveness and, especially, the frictions and conflictual dynamics of the "mutuality of being"/relational consubstantiality.

of the sister's child by the mother's brother.[4] Although performed clandestinely, this is both a "last resort" and a fully normative act of destruction within the nucleus of kinship—the matrifilial circuitry. The act consists of a spell incantation over a piece of pork that represents the bodily flesh of the sister's child. The child's flesh derives from the maternal uncle's (qua his sister's) generative embodiment of their common (self-same) paternal bone. In other words, a disgruntled MB, when deprived of his rightful payments, will destroy his own substantial self-same *difference* embodied in his sister's child's (ZCh) flesh. This is rendered even more explicit in the person of the ZS whose name, incarnated in his flesh, is axiomatically his mother's *latice*

---

4. This malediction is the prerogative of the "base" or the "root" male mother, thus one's mother's true brother who as such is of the same birth order as his sister (that means, ego's mother; for the Yagwoia birth-order system, see Mimica 1988, 1991). When this MB dies, he is succeeded as the "base" MB by his first-born son (MBS). All other real MBs (i.e., not of the same birth order as one's mother) are so to speak less "basal" than the same-birth order MB. In the context of death payments, the base MB is expected to be a taciturn presence; he, and also his brothers and sisters, are not supposed to make any loud demands for their due payments, which are expected to be the largest, more so if some of them take upon themselves to bury their ZCh. By contrast, the classificatory mothers' (male and female) behavior in the same context is characterized by loud lamenting, an ostentatious display of anger, and complaining when they are dissatisfied with the payments they receive. Their display of outrage and loss may include breaking the garden and homestead fences of those kin of the deceased who are responsible for the distribution of the payments. A person's actual mother, on the other hand, is held to have a direct influence on one (one's soul) especially while still a young child, which makes one especially vulnerable if separated from her. A mother's thinking about her absent child will arrest its growth.

(bone) name (Mimica 1991). Accordingly, in the spell the maternal uncle first pronounces his own name, which, being that of his own mother's *laṭice*, is different from that of his own bone-substance embodied by his ZCh as his flesh self-substance, the target of the MB's destructive action. Then the MB pronounces his ZCh's name, that is, his own bone-substance and patri-name.[5] As my informant explained, if the maternal uncle does not make that differentiation, he may easily destroy himself, for the spell will rebound back on himself.

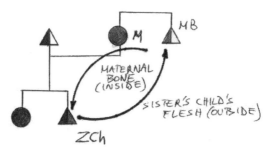

Figure 2. Yagwoia naming system and the MB^ZS name inversion

In the actual situation of our original communication, my informant insisted that the two of us be seated with our backs turned toward each other so that we would not look at each other's face (a situation of exceptional significance, as we shall see below).[6] Since I had to ask

---

5. Parenthetically, in this self-differentiation of the MB paternal bone, which via his sister's embodiment becomes her child's (that is, ZCh's) bodily flesh envelope, a particular ouroboric exo > < endo dynamics is manifest. Through numerous self-permutations, this dynamic undergoes differentiations constitutive of the Yagwoia social field in its entirety (Mimica 1991).

6. This is a common position when any grave *ki'nye ququna yakale* is imparted.

him to repeat the spell several times in order that I could write it down correctly, I had to look at his face, especially the movements of his mouth, a libidinally highly charged orifice for the Yagwoia. My informant became so upset by my behavior that he burst into tears, saying that we were talking too much about a truly bad activity. His distress was due to the subject matter itself, for the mother's breast's (i.e., MB) curse is truly a radical malignancy immanent in the matrifilial kinship. Only because of this commanding generative^destructive immanence does the maternal uncle have the life^death power over his ZCh; and it alone ensures that the life payments due from the ZCh to the MB will be made, by hook or by crook. Most importantly, this act cannot be performed in reverse: that is, even if the ZCh wanted to, he/she cannot use the same spell to destroy his/her maternal uncle because the ZCh is void of that immanent power of being the source of his/her own life. Nor can the ZCh undo the effect of the act; only the MB can do so. A man can always and only do it to his own sister's child. This is why the curse of the maternal uncle is not the same as the spells and associated substances and gestures used in regular *ki'nye*.

If one were to look for an instance of willful malignancy constitutive of their intersubjectivity that for the very reason could be rendered as a paradigmatic example of what in the Western tradition pertains to the problematic of "human evil," then this is the most apposite one. But as an expression of its ouroboric determination, this willful malignancy has to be seen for what it is—the principial coercive moral nucleus of kinship, itself the matrixial medium of life^death. *What drives this morality is the death-inflicting intentionality.* However, this ouroboric dynamics of the Yagwoia body social—their collective (un)conscious and the cultural imaginary as a whole—require some internal amplification in reference to the overall configuration of specifically their cannibalistic practices and the correlative moral (ethos) and hedonic sensibilities *borne out of the facticity of the bodily generation of human life.*[7] It is not a "free gift" but a product of the self-loss, the rupture of the self-unity and fullness of the cosmogonic ouroboric self-unity replicated in every woman's being, namely her ouroboric (phallic) womb that binds her and her brother in their common paternal cross-sex-self-unity; that is, begotten by the same parents (F^M), the B^Z couple is the full embodiment (identical bone and flesh) of their mutual contra-sexual identity. Correspondingly, a ZCh's bodily life is the inalienable possession of its absolute

---

7. A similar determining role of the death-inflicting intentionality directed at one's own kind is intimated in the Trobriand tradition concerning the origin and practice of the deadliest form of sorcery (Malinowski [1922] 1966, 74): "It is a firm and definite belief among all the natives that if a man's sorcery has to be any good, it must first be practiced on his mother or sister, or any of his maternal kindred. Such a matricidal act makes him a genuine *bwaga'u*. His art then can be practiced on others, and becomes an established source of income." In a sense, in order to become a master killer, which implies being the master of life^death, one has to kill if not oneself directly then someone who is virtually the same as oneself (note here the close parallel to becoming a *sanguma* and/or a shaman—as reported by Mitchell (1975), Elkin (1964), and Warner (1958). This in my view implies that sorcery presupposes a maximum degree of autonomy articulated through the killing of one's life-giver or her closest equivalent. The power to kill derives from the life-giving power. More correctly, it can be interpreted as a single power that, turned against itself, is transformed into its negative positivity. In the Trobriands (Malinowski [1922] 1966), it was the crab who originally brought sorcery from the south. It was visibly within the crab, for it was red. The dog saw it and tried to bite it. In turn the crab killed it. Then the crab killed a man but, feeling sorry for him, revived him (here the power of killing is conterminous with reviving). The man offered the crab a large payment (*pokala*) for the latter to show him the magic. The crab did this, and the man immediately used it to kill the crab.

possessor—the female^male mothers (i.e., its M and MB) and it is through them that the ZCh is the possession of all of its other "male and female mothers" (e.g., MZ, MBS, MBD, MBSS, MBSD).

Planted, as it is, by my father, my body comes into being in and at the expense of my mother's body, the embodiment of and conduit (through her skeleton) for her paternal bone-generativity. In this osseous determination, my mother is my MB's ouroboric (phallic) womb and as such is also the tomb for my flesh in more than one mode. The fullness (wellbeing) of my bodily life (flesh) is correlative with the fullness of my mothers' mouth = stomach, principally that of my mother's same-birth order brother, my principial "mother's breast." In case my life-payments are not forthcoming (i.e., no life-substance goes via his mouth into his stomach), sooner or later his privation will come to plague me, as the wounds and bodily flesh self-loss inflicted by him on me. That is, I am thereby eaten back alive but in a negative, rather than in a positive, life-sustaining, and enhancing mode. The curse is the negative, death-dispensing disposition of the selfsame maternal life^death power circuit that sustains the life of the bodily flesh.

In the edifice of the Yagwoia world-body, this is the negative actualization of the specifically lunar effluence that, in conjunction with the sun's circular motion, generates the primary thermal effluence (*umpne*) without which the substance of the world-body would not be what it is, that is, generative of its own life. In the concrete human embodiment (microcosmos), this luno-solar effluence is generated through the intra-bodily motions of the bone marrow (the solar-paternal quiddity, the source of semen and breast milk) and blood (the lunar-maternal quiddity). Both substances, like the whole of the body, are continuously generated through the eating of the substantiality of the world-body. The point of this synoptic discussion is to illustrate the cosmo-ontological ambivalence of libido^mortido immanent in the dynamics of the Yagwoia intersubjectivity and its moral articulation.[8] This explanation of the mother's breast's malediction now allows a brief elucidation of the work of *ki'nye*.

Sorcery in hindsight

As I already emphasized, there is no "sorcery" without the immanent powers of those words that are *ququne yakale* (spells). These, however, are not human volitional creations but are received from wild forest spirits in visionary experiences and, through dreams, from the base (*qaule*) ancestors of particular *latice* groups. In that case it is the persons who are the "bone" members of these groups, by that very bodily determination, who can and do bring maximally into effect the powers of such spells. On the other hand, spells and associated rites can be bought and sold; even if they are of a different language (i.e., speech-substance), their power is nonetheless contained in them. Furthermore, in the case of destructive spells-acts, their power is volatile and, relative to their gravity, they have to be handled with extreme care; the most destructive ones, as we shall see in a moment, require, so to speak, a "mirror-self" approach.

As I pointed out in the above example, my informant did not want me to face him and vice versa. For the Yagwoia, looking face-to-face is a salient archetypal image of a perfect (absolute) symmetry and parity. It is here that the articulation of their sense of equality and its differentiation into good and bad, justice and injustice, and other modalities of self-world valuation—that is, the constitution of intersubjectivity as an immanently value-laden field

---

8. In Mimica (1991) I show how this nuclear death^life negativity that constitutes matrifilial circuity is but an aspect of the self-totalizing ouroboric desire that drives incest dynamics, which in turn generates the entire field of Yagwoia kinship praxis and the social institutions formed upon it.

of relatedness—can be informatively developed.[9] In the face-to-face situation, I and you face = look-at-each-other (in the Yagwoia language, looking is predicated as ocular eating, i.e., in the oral = ocular register) and therefore are in perfect mutual self-symmetry that determines reciprocity as a dynamic mirror-structure. Immanent in it is the mirror-self-difference: the mirror shows one's self-semblance that is, imperceptibly, self-inverted. Further, modalization of this ocular-oral-facial self-symmetry occurs at the level of the genital-anal zone (Mimica 1981: 88–93; 1991: 43–45). Briefly, this lower level of the body is conceived as the facial gestalt in which the genital "face" (male and female) is bivalent: for example, offering one's genitals can be, verbally or de facto, relative to the intention and the situation, either a positive or a negative gesture. By contrast, the invocation/comportment of the anal "face" is primarily negative.

The most potent expression of this is in the performance of a truly lethal *ki'nye* act, in which the sorcerer walks backward with the sorcery substance impaled on a stick (i.e., not handled by direct manual contact) and carried behind the back, in front of the anus, while the sorcery spell is muttered through the mouth. In this action, however, the oral orifice is displaced onto the "*ilyce malye*" (faeces lips, i.e., the outer rim of the anus). In this way the malignancy of the act is deflected from the front-face, that is, the egoic focus of the sorcerer, to his posterior that as such is his mirror-inverted egoity and therefore not *exactly* his-self. In other words, he is the perpetrator of the act, and yet his agency is attenuated: qua his posterior, he is to himself a mirror-self-other and, therefore, protected from the malignancy that is literally generated through his desire, volition, and action.

---

9. This scheme is derived from the mother-child incorporative^excorporative self-circuity articulated in the Yagwoia matrifilial kinship and the life-cycle exchange (see Mimica 1991).

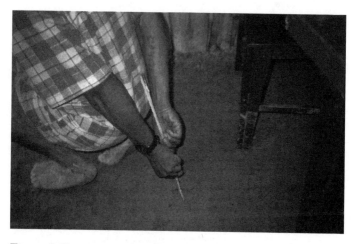

Figure 3. Doing *ki'nye* (sorcery)

However, this use of the "hind-face" gestalt is not just due to the fact that the anus is regarded as an exclusively evacuating/rejecting (i.e., inside > outside) orifice.[10] Unlike the frontal-genital zone that is coterminous with the upper head-face endowed with the two eyes and the mouth-nose (these orifices are self-symmetrical in relation to the inside-outside projection, i.e., their dynamics is reversible— inside > outside > inside), the backside zone is eye-less. Accordingly, by facing something with one's behind one does not face the world with the receptive ocular surface but with the eyeless "hind-face" gestalt that does not look at, and therefore does not introject, its object. Unlike the mouth, the anus is exclusively a rejecting orifice and so the behind does not have a chance to introjectively self-identify with such ocular equivalents as penis and hand. The human face, being oral and ocular, does so willy-nilly. That is why one may be compelled to close, cover, or avert the eyes when facing a repelling sight. Hind-face does not, for

---

10. For an example in the context of mortuary practices, see Mimica (2003a).

it has no eyes, and although the anus is highly constrictive, when in fright or shock it is more likely to let go of itself. *In the performance of a ki'nye act, the actor is protected precisely because he is not looking at, that is, ingesting back into himself, the instrumental object of his activity and is for that reason less liable to be affected by the malignancy that he thereby actualizes.* I should say that this pronouncedly negative valorization of the anal zone in the Yagwoia lifeworld is clearly conditioned by the hyper-valorization of the oral-mammary zone, which simultaneously assimilates the genital. It is a pure expression of the primary phallo-oral-ocular nucleus of the ouroboric embodiment.[11]

These body-focused aspects of *ki'nye* activity will have to suffice as an illustration of the problematic of "sorcery" vis-à-vis other modalities of the soul's malignant capacity and its macrocosmic spirit(ual) matrix. Only on the basis of these considerations can one adequately account for Yagwoia intersubjectivity and sociality as a moral field with differential configurations and distributions of culpability. This field was never and still is not *in toto* subjected, despite all the work of Christian missions, to such cosmo-ontological polarization as radical good and evil and a correlative

---

11. In some other New Guinea lifeworlds, where symptomatically the institutionalized male homosexual practices are centered on exclusive anal contact, the anus has positive libidinal charge: it is an ingesting-incorporative orifice. In regard to the male bodily-zonal bisexual mapping, the anus is commonly rendered as a female—vaginal—orifice and as such is used in kinship classification. For instance, among the Kamoro-Mimika (Pouwer 1966, 2010), man discriminates between his own children as the ones "of his penis" and his sister's children as the ones "of his anus." Among the Kaluli (Schieffelin 1976), spirit familiars enter the spirit mediums through their anuses. On the other hand, there are Melanesian lifeworlds, such as in New Ireland (Eves 1995), where spirit-powers can penetrate the human body through all orifices, irrespective of what the normative psycho-sexual preference(s) may be.

project of salvation. On par with the ouroboric facticity of their lifeworld, it has been void of both heaven and hell for the last 60,000 years; herein, the ouroboric life^death process of ceaseless existence reigns supreme and generates neither the promise of eternal salvation nor damnation (Mimica 2003a). Hence comes the reason why the fate of Christianity, like everything else that the Western world system has hitherto brought into the Yagwoia lifeworld, can only be adequately understood within the purview of the dynamics and the problematic of so many affections and afflictions that befall their souls. Accordingly, within the interiority of the Yagwoia lifeworld and its world-body, the macrocosmic container that generates all its contents, Christianity has to be approached as a problematic and, in so many cases, a transient rather than a permanent affection and/or affliction of the soul.

CHAPTER 6

The womba complex in regional perspective

In order to gain a deeper perspective on the cannibalistic womba complex in its primary unadulterated and unsublimated core, it is helpful to place it into the larger context of the Angan and the external Highlands region. As far as the Yagwoia facts are concerned, what matters is that among them no confirmed womba or simple sufferer of the dream visions that may turn a person into one runs the risk of being killed by fellow villagers for that reason. This sharply contrasts with their Menya-speaking neighbors, the Pataye, who readily kill persons (male and female, infants and adults) identified, usually by shamans, as womba. During my 1984–86 fieldwork stint, I received occasional reports from Menyamya that corpses of killed womba had been found in the Kwotayi and Wapi rivers or that some Menya individuals (commonly very young children and adolescents), accused of being womba, sought protection at the Lutheran and/or SDA mission stations, for otherwise they would have been killed. A number of such unfortunate Pataye persons, mostly women but also young individuals and children of either sex, have also sought refuge among the Iqwaye and Hyaqwangilyce Yagwoia. Unperturbed by their soul-condition, the Iqwaye accept these individuals and, commonly, the women are adopted, which means looked after and renamed. When they get married, their adoptive fathers and brothers duly receive the bride-price. The distinctive value of these women is that their adoption does not involve any payments to their original agnatic or maternal relations. Thus, should some of their Pataye relatives come to claim a payment or even the bride-price, they are packed off: "Aiiy!!? You first wanted to kill her and now you ask for a payment?! Go back to your place!"

The non-Angan outsiders

The following case illustrates succinctly the tolerant Yagwoia attitude toward the womba condition. A man, married to a Simbu woman and living with his affines in Goroka for the better part of his adult life, reported upon one of his visits to his home area that he participated in the killing of a woman accused of being a witch (*sanguma*). He stated that she was proven to be so when submitted to a test: when a can of intact tinned fish was placed in front of her, she (i.e., her soul) managed to completely eat its contents while the can remained unopened. This led to her execution: the unfortunate woman was killed by a red-hot iron rod driven through the junction of her neck and shoulders. His father was quite dismayed to hear this, but the son defended himself by saying that he followed the custom of his affines. What is more, he said, when they reported the killing to the police, the latter congratulated them on their good work. The dead woman's group did not demand compensation because this does not apply to killed *sanguma* persons. The event took place sometime between 1995 and 1998.[1] By

---

1. The man also averred that the settlements in Goroka are swelling with *sanguma* and that all *sanguma* have a king and a queen. He made the point that unlike "here" (his home area), there are no persons in Goroka who command other spirit

contrast, his father expressed the local attitudes when he said that the son should have brought this woman "here" (his home place) so that a local shaman could have got rid of her womba soul affliction, and that would be it. In fact, the father stated, he himself had the womba affliction but very quickly managed to expel it from his soul.

In 1992 two teachers who worked at a local community school came to stay with me for two days. The senior of the two, the school's headmaster, was from the Lufa area in the Eastern Highlands province (not far from Goroka). In the course of a series of long conversations, he described how *sanguma* were a problem in his home area. He had organized and conducted the trial of a woman who, through a methodical examination (i.e., torture; she was tied and suspended by her hands on a wire and then exposed to controlled burning), confessed that she was a *sanguma*. She was then killed. He emphasized that throughout the process a man wrote down in a notebook everything that they had asked of her and, of course, her replies. The point he wanted to make was that, with him being an educated person, they followed a proper order of investigation on the model of the court of law.

---

powers, only the womba kind (i.e., he identified it with the Tok Pisin *sanguma*). As for the Simbu and the Highlands, he said that there is a huge cliff called the Helembari Stone (possibly the conical rocky peak of Mount Wilhelm) that is the gathering place of all Highlands *sanguma*—"their House of Parliament." He likened it to the local, though much smaller, Tamauwye cliff, a dwelling favored by the wild forest spirits (*hyaqaye ilymane*). In the same breath he likened both Helembari Stone and Tamauwye to the Yagwoia ritual house (*inekiye*) due to the latter's connection with the wild spirits, the source of various soul powers, and, as the largest house constructed by the Yagwoia, its association with a parliament. For the Simbu "*Kumo* witchcraft," see Aufenanger (1965), Brown (1977), Hughes (1985, 1988), Gibbs (2012), and Zocca (2009).

Reverberations of the complex among neighboring Angan groups

The Yagwoia hold a view that some groups as a whole are womba cannibals: as it were, everyone without exception has that sort of malignant cannibalistic potency. In this respect Hiwoye, who was one of my main coworkers over many years, thought that the reason why there are so many womba among the Paṭaye and other Menya-speaking groups has to do with the kind of *himace* power-objects specific to these groups, objects that came into existence with the birth of the world. In this view the malignant potency is immanent among these people, which by the same token would imply that this is also the reason as to why the Pataye attitude toward the womba is lethal while that of the Yagwoia is not. Qang thought that, perhaps, Paṭaye may fear that their womba would exterminate them, therefore they preempt such an eventuality by killing them.

Concerning this sort of group-pervasive womba immanence, it is their southern neighbors, the Ankave-speaking Yaqauwye in the interior of the Gulf province, who reign supreme.[2] They are all and invariably womba, which is why so many Yagwoia are not all that keen on frequenting this area. They have links to the Yaqauwye because the latter are not salt-makers and obtain this from the Yagwoia

---

2. Lemonnier and Bonnemère have done extensive ethnographic work among the Yaqauwye (see, e.g., Bonnemère 2018; Bonnemère and Lemonnier 2007). Regarding the Yaqauwye womba complex (*ombi'* in Ankave), the definitive account is Lemonnier's (2006) *Le sabbat des lucioles: sorcellerie, chamanisme et imaginaire cannibale en Nouvelle-Guinee* (The sabbath of the fireflies: Sorcery, shamanism, and cannibal imaginary in New Guinea). A short but informative account in English is his 1998 article. The group with whom he and Bonnemère primarily work, live in the upper Mbewi river; the area where their hamlets are located is known among the Yagwoia as Iqumdi (Ikundi in Lemonnier's writings).

in exchange for tapa. In this respect, the Yagwoia regard themselves as being especially covetous to the Yaqauwye as their flesh is more tasty since they eat salt more frequently and in larger amounts.

The following exemplifies how readily Yagwoia see virtually any experience made among the Yaqauwye as due to a womba attempt at their flesh. On his first visit ever to Iqumdi, Hi-Caqauwye noticed when waking up after his first night there that the shoulder-string of his net bag was broken. He wondered whether it might have been a mouse that did this, but his companions told him that it must have been some local womba. During the second night he was unable to sleep because cockroaches (*wona'uwye*) kept on disturbing him. When he returned home his father explained these events: the cockroaches were actually the manifestation of his soul whereby he was kept awake and, therefore, not exposed to a womba attack. As for the broken string of his net bag, this too was the work of a womba: evidently repelled by his soul, the womba had nothing else to bite, as it were, but the net bag. Hi-Caqauwye's father made the point that by protecting him against the notorious Yaqauwye menace, his soul was indeed proven to be very strong.

Before pacification, the Yagwoia territorial group Ng-Wa:ce was completely routed by the Iqwaye and the Menya-speaking Pataye; they sought refuge among the Yaqauwye and, because of that, have become almost like their hosts. In the wake of pacification, the Ng-Wa:ce reoccupied most of their original territory except for the sectors taken over by the Pataye—a source of ongoing land disputes. But the legacy of their residence with the Yaqauwye has been that there are now too many womba among the Ng-Wa:ce. In the mid-1990s one of them made no secret that he was a womba and tried to mobilize his fellow Ng-W:ace to get rid of their malignant Yaqauwye inheritance on a collective scale. The man's call did not result in any action, but his case provides a glimpse into a new development within the Yagwoia womba imaginary. I obtained the relevant information from Qang who visited this man, Ma-Nguye, at his home place.

According to Ma-Nguye there are not just a few womba individuals but entire covens of them with leaders. Among the Ng-Wa:ce he was the leader and this is why he wanted to organize a purge because there were too many womba and, presumably because he was also a shaman, he did not like it. The cleansing would have required that all womba publicly surrender their razor-sharp bamboo knives with which they cut pork and human flesh. Divested of their nefarious instruments that would now be in the open for everyone to see, Ma-Nguve seems to have assumed, their power would also be extinguished. The womba knife is decorated with a *qwapiye ungopace* (White Man's ribbon, i.e., industrial strip of textile). It is located in the womba's head (face-side) and is handled by his *kune–umpne* soul. Another implement is a human hand that the womba has severed from a victim and incorporated into his womba body. His soul controls the hand by means of strings so that it can emerge at will through his regular hand. Ma-Nguye detailed this in reference to the Ankave-speaking Yaquwye and Kauwyase groups. He said that when an outsider visits them and the local womba try to cannibalize him, his Ankave host will protect him by scolding and challenging his fellow womba-villagers: "Let me see how many men did you kill?! You count yours [victims] and I'll count mine!" He will then produce the hand from inside his body in such a manner that his normal hand will swell up as the inner one is emerging through it while hanging on the strings. "Have you got this kind of power so you want to kill my friend?!" Then he will withdraw the hand back into his body. This will be a strong enough display to deter the other womba.

Ma-Nguye said that he also has this kind of third hand, thus reasserting his position as a womba leader. Moreover it seems that it is the leaders who are the principal slashers of human flesh because they wear a special uniform for that purpose, like a "*saintist*" (pidginized form of "scientist") and a "*dokta*" (doctor), that is, a coat. They do the cutting and distribute the flesh to their fellow womba. This clearly indicates that the major source of the new components in the Yagwoia womba imaginary are the Western institutions of the hospital and the morgue as well as the general regimented order of relations at work in any government organization. In the hospital context, it is doctors and surgeons who are the "boss" or "leader"; the followers are nurses and other staff. The Ng-Wa:ce womba knife invokes medical associations: it combines the traditional bamboo blade with the "White Man's ribbon" that echoes an image of the scalpel while the mobile hand may well be inspired by a contraption such as a prosthetic arm.[3] Regardless of such

---

3. I am not surprised to read that, for instance, among the Asaro and Bena groups in the Eastern Highlands people have reconfigured their images of witches through the influence of Western vampire movies (e.g., Strong 2017; Knapp 2017). Regarding the mobile extra arm, a phallic-aggressive (protensive^ retracting) aspect of this Yagwoia image is quite apparent. Although it may well be that it was inspired by such a Western medical contraption as a prosthetic limb cum a surgeon's scalpel, I believe that it is also conditioned by the dominant Yagwoia phallic body-image most acutely and manifestly expressed in the traditional multi-layered male grass-apron that simultaneously conceals and makes the genital zone conspicuously pronounced (Mimica 1981, 135–39). It projects a narcissistic image of male embodiment in the state of permanent erection, hence of a virility always ready to execute its life^death power (*yeki'/t/nye*). This type of multilayered male apron is common to virtually all Angan groups. As a component of the womba gestalt, this image of bodily power is transfigured into a singular menacing instrument of destruction. Although I shared Qang's sentiment about this image of a third mobile slasher-hand (he was shaking with fear when he first learnt about it), it also reminded me of Rolf Harris's famous song, "I'm Jake the

likely influences, the authorship of these novel elaborations (mobile knife, hand, and covens) is clearly credited to the Yagwoia's southern neighbors Ankave from where derives Ma-Nguye's womba soul-power.[4] He also told Qang that womba covens exist in other Yagwoia groups, specifically mentioning the Iwolaqa-Malycaane and Iqwayaane, as well as the Menya-speaking Patayaane. But, so it seems, the local people do not know that these covens exist in their midst.

Qang's response to this account was quite revealing of what can be taken as the general wily attitude toward life, including the womba phenomenon, so characteristic of the Yagwoia. He sincerely acknowledged that such details as the mobile knife and hand and the fact that these womba form covens, "like an army" (he commented), made him shiver. Nevertheless he asked his womba interlocutor the following question: "Given that there are so many of you [i.e., the militarily organized Ng-Wa:ce womba with their knife powers and the leader with a mobile hand], why don't you kill all the [Menya-speaking] Pataye who have been taking over your lands for so long?" Qang was referring to the endless land conflicts between the Ng-Wa:ce and the Pataye, which neither the Australian nor the PNG government were able resolve. In consequence, since pacification the Pataye have been by far the most successful predatory and expansionist group in the region. Ma-Nguye replied as follows: "How can you kill them off and rout them when they too have got their boss [i.e., they are organized and have the same powers]? There is their

---

Peg, diddle-iddle-iddle um/With my extra leg, diddle-iddle-iddle-um/...."

4. This parallels three Iwolaqa-Malyce (Yagwoia) shamans who acquired their shamanistic powers, manifest in the specific styles of healing technique and the use of trance and singing, from their Simbari and Baruya neighbors, that is from the wild forest spirits dwelling in these territories.

boss and you can't eradicate him!"[5] What transpires from Qang's account is that his interlocutor did not see the womba condition as an absolutely undesirable affliction of the soul but as a power that has a value and, so it seems, primarily as a means of showing off and inspiring fear that effects no instrumental action of consequence, certainly not of the kind that Qang's questioning suggested—fighting a predatory group.

A comparative amplification

A reflection is in order at this junction. Qang's questioning brings to mind the phenomenon of "spiritual warfare" exemplified, for instance, by Amazonian shamanistic practices (e.g., Lizot (1985) 1991; Jokic 2015; Overing 1986). Yagwoia are mindful of the lethal powers that some of their neighbors possess (e.g., the Ankave speaking Yaqauwye) and there are instances of attacks and ensuing misfortunes due to extraterritorial, non-Yagwoia shamans and sorcerers. But neither in the past nor at present are there scenarios where male and female shamans with their spirits would systematically act together to defend their group territory from attack by enemy shamans and, in turn, attack these, with their ordinary fellow villagers remaining unaware of these nocturnal shamanic pursuits. Godelier (1986: 114–16) describes such a scenario of nocturnal covens of male and female shamans in his account of the functional features of Baruya shamanism while A. Strathern (1994: 290–92) further schematized it for the purpose of his comparative survey of "shamanism and politics" in Papua New Guinea.

---

5. It should be noted in this connection that, unlike the Yagwoia who do not see the womba in their midst as a mortal threat, the Pataye do so and act accordingly, possibly exactly because the kind of peril that Qang formulated as a situation can be advantageous to their factual, external enemies.

The Baruya-speaking Angans are Yagwoias' northern neighbors. As for their approximate equivalent of the Yagwoia womba, Godelier (1986: 114–15, 116) says that "the shamans themselves are witches" and on some occasions "their spirits roam above the territory in broad daylight, and they sometimes enter the body of a Baruya and devour his or her liver." This "baneful power" is involuntary. It is not clear from his account how shamans acquire it. Somewhat in a roundabout manner he writes that "[w]omen and children are particularly vulnerable to this kind of involuntary aggression, which is less a matter of sorcery proper than of what the Anglo-Saxons call witchcraft, an evil activity, taking the form of a power of death that emanates from some individual independently of his or her will" (Godelier 1986: 116). Although a witch-shaman could use this power against their fellow Baruya, "it is totally forbidden." Moreover, shamans "regard themselves, and they are regarded, as being in the service of the community" (Godelier 1986: 115).

I will pursue some implications of this situation in reference to A. Strathern (1994: 288) who remarks on the ambivalence of shamanic powers by likening it to the organization of Tiv lineage leadership in Nigeria (Bohannan [1957] 1968: 162–64). This African transposition will amplify the inner problematic of Baruya shamanism. The Tiv leadership comprises male elders who "repair" (meaning governing and spiritually protecting) lineage territories (*tar*). "The elders who repair the *tar* by day—what we could call secular governing—form, Tiv say, an organization which meets at night in order to carry out secret rituals for the religious protection of the community. As such, they are called 'the *mbatsav*', those with talent" (Bohannan [1957] 1968: 162–63). Bohannan accentuates this diurnal/nocturnal dichotomy by saying that these "influential elders of the community 'by day' are said to be the 'witches' by night." But he immediately follows this up with: "'Witches' is not a good translation of *mbatsav*, even in the light only of other African data. Leadership—indeed, all ability—is an attribute, Tiv say, of a substance called *tsav* that grows on the heart of some men. A man of *tsav* (*or tsav*) is a man of talent. The talent includes mystical power" (Bohannan [1957] 1968: 162). However, these individuals

> are 'dangerous' (*kwaghbo*); they are feared; they are also trusted. In times of political upheaval, the trust disappears. As Tiv put it, the *mbatsav* begin to use their talent to kill for personal gain and *for the sheer love of the taste of human flesh*. Tiv revolt always takes the form of anti-*tsav* uprisings. This usually means that the revolt is directed against the most influential elders of the community, who are 'by night' the *mbatsav*. In peaceful times, the *mbatsav* of the community protect its members from evil and from the *mbatsav* of other communities. That is the reason why times are peaceful. But protectors of the community have license to destroy its individual members for purposes considered legitimate and for the good of all. (Bohannan [1957] 1968: 163, emphasis added).

Considered psychoanalytically, the (un)conscious matrix of the Tiv cultural imaginary constituting their system of "political" power is an ambivalent libido^destrudo equilibrium precariously balanced as a differential self^non-self administration of life^death inside and outside of their body social. To use a bio-medical image, the equilibrium is intrinsically predisposed toward autoimmune disorder and, eventually, it starts attacking itself, that is, turns autophagous: "Tiv see leaders in two lights: as their protectors and as their eventual vanquishers" (Bohannan, [1957] 1968: 163). Reflecting now on the Baruya situation, their shamans are "totally forbidden" to give vent to the cannibalistic desire of their souls, Godelier writes, but he does not say how this interdiction is imposed on their spirits given that this is an involuntary disposition. When compared with the Yagwoia, the Baruya variant of the womba malignancy seems to be exclusive to the spirits of shamans, but because of its beneficial function this malignancy does not make womba open to deadly persecutions. This is different from the way that the Menya-speaking Paṭaye deal with their womba, identified as such by shamans yet accepted (i.e., adopted and married) by the opportunistic Iqwaye and Hyaqwangilyce Yagwoia into their ouroboric body social wherein anybody's soul can be tempted by the womba desire but not everyone is likely to succumb to it. When disclosed to consociates it is open to shamanic treatment and, even if not fully extinguished, is subject to neutralization. In the image of autoimmune system dynamics, the Yagwoia social body is most efficacious in metabolizing the womba malignancy whose "political" value, either negative or positive, is nil, but especially in the female embodiment of the Menya-speaking refugees it is a source of singular financial gain, since their adopted protectors, turned agnates, claim the whole of bride-price.

At this juncture it is constructive to take a retrospective look at Yagwoia gender dynamics qua the womba complex. When the complex is seen in relation to its refractions and resonances among their neighbors, it becomes evident that the Yagwoia do tolerate and, indeed, metabolize quite effectively this internal modality of their cannibalistic desires without persecuting either women or men. The fact that I recorded no case of a Yagwoia woman who was tormented by the womba experience and thereby prompted to talk out and seek shamanic treatment does not mean that there were (or are) no such cases. Moreover, if there were, that is not memorable per se, especially if these experiences ceased or the person can handle them. If Qang himself did not tell me about his experience when I inquired about the womba condition, in all probability nobody else would have done so either, precisely because it was of no memorable consequence, neither for his wives and children. What is memorable about the two womba-women who were killed is that their womba-hood was manifested in the pig form:

they were destroying gardens (not human life) and as such they got killed. These two cases are particularly expressive of the Yagwoia cultural imaginary and the inner nexus between womba, female pig identity, and the desire for pork, the latter being the equipollent stirrings in both the men's and women's souls.

Then, given this factuality of the Yagwoia womba complex, a balanced assessment of the manifest difference in its gender expression is that there is no grave intersubjective stigma that would pressure either men or women to deal with their actual womba experiences unless the person himself/ herself felt gravely threatened by them. And when they do talk out, this is to their kin primarily for the kind of reasons that Qang gave in his self-account, namely that he cared about his wives and children. With OMitane, if nothing else the overwhelming impact of his womba showings was that neither he nor his favorite wife, who always attended to him, could get a good night's sleep. Whatever the outcome of the shamanic treatment may be in any given case (male or female), this per se does not necessarily translate into a memorable social fact. And the efficiency of the cure, that is, getting rid of the affliction, critically depends on the person's wish and will—the soul's endeavor—to get rid of it (exemplified well by OAp).

As to why these Yagwoia men, whom I got to know, were motivated by their womba experiences to talk out and seek treatment, it is clearly conditioned by the very intensity of their womba showings and the suffering that these bring, as well as the moral sense of caring for the wellbeing of their immediate kin. Correlatively, there is a concern with how they may be seen by their fellow villagers (e.g., Qang's statements) but this does not lead into a dramatic concern with or collapse of one's self-image and status in the intersubjective field or a dire existential threat.[6] This is

---

6. OMitane, for instance, could not care less as to how he might be seen by his fellow villagers on account of his womba

just as true of any woman who, in the context of domestic disgruntlements, may be said by her husband (or co-wives) to be a womba-woman who eats her own children. Regardless of the actual affective force with which this may be stated, it does not have any grave "public" effect, so that framing this specifically female aspect of the complex as a significantly persecutory (women by men) instance of gender—qua womba—tension would unduly push the Yagwoia womba complex into the anthropological frame of "witchcraft confessions and accusations," that is, a distorting stereotyping.

Ankavi *ombi'* and the Yagwoia womba

I will now return to the problematic of the womba situation among the Ankave-Angan speakers from where historically the Ng-Wa:ce-Yagwoia received both the malignancy (from their former Yaqauwye hosts) and, more recently, such hitherto unknown features as womba covens and "bosses" with knives and mobile third hands, as revealed to Qang by Ma-NGuye, a shaman and self-avowed womba leader who wanted to exorcise his confreres' malignancy. To be sure, this image is one created by the Yagwoia on the basis of their experience of interaction with these *ulyce* (foreign-speaking and distant) groups. As for the situation among the Ankave, irrespective of its transfigurations within the Yagwoia womba imaginary, Lemonnier's accounts (1998,

---

predicament. The narcissistic equilibrium of Yagwoia egoity and its gradient of (in)vulnerability and resilience form a dynamic structure considerably different and, in some respects, more robust than the ego-self systems of Western megapolitan good citizens and, especially, of those among them whose souls are primed by a Christian ethos and an existential orientation to the W/holy Other.

2006) give a different picture, of which I will give only a few diacritical details.[7]

By comparison to other Angan groups that surround them, the Ankave were historically and still are a small, marginal, and vulnerable population, ecologically, politically (both in terms of inter-tribal relations and towards the PNG state), and bio-medically—especially in terms of malaria.[8]

---

7. There is a beautifully illustrated bilingual book by Bonnemère and Lemonnier (2007: 192–206) that contains some relevant information on the Ankave *ombi'*. Here, I primarily draw on Lemonnier's "Showing the Invisible" paper that provides a synopsis of the Ankave situation both in the regions of Iqumdi (Yaqauwye or NW Ankave) and among the groups in Mbuli and Angayi (Central Ankave) (Lemonnier 1998: esp. 296–302).

8. One of the best examples of Ankave marginality is the way they were historically cheated in intertribal trade by the two main salt-making Yagwoia groups (Iqwaye and Iwolaqa-Malyce). When dealing with the Yaqauwye (NW Ankave), the salt traders mixed salt with bamboo sawdust to a proportion of 3:5. This went on until the Yagwoia-Ng-Wa:ce territorial group was routed by the Iqwaye and the Menya-speaking Pataye military alliance that forced the former to seek refuge among the Yaqauwye (between 1940 and 1951, i.e., when the Menyamya Patrol station was established). The refugees revealed to their hosts how the Iqwaye and Iwolaqa-Malyce had been ripping them off. But they added: "Now your *katouqwa* [older brother, i.e., the Ng-Wa:ce] has come to stay with you, so we'll look after you." I learned about this from one of my Iwolaqa-Malyce informants who, having recounted the story, lamented the consequence of Ng-Wa:ce betrayal as follows: "Why did they do it?! We [the Yagwoia salt makers] used to fool the Yaqauwye so well, all to our advantage, but the Ng-Wa:ce ruined it all!" This sort of inclination towards cheating in trade was uniformly applied in all their dealings with the southern Angan groups in the interior of Gulf province, although the primary link in the trade chain ensuing from the Yagwoia were Yaqauwye.

According to their ethnographers, Ankave *ombi'* are a special and the most dreaded class of spirits whose cosmogonic origin is conterminous with humans (Bonnemère and Lemonnier 2007: 192).[9] They are "cannibal spirits living inside a human host (male or female, adult or child) who directs them. They attack those against whom their master has some grievance" (Lemonnier 1998: 296). "The *ombi'* outnumber the Ankave and gather deep in the forest to feast on the bodies of those they have killed. When they appear in human form, these monsters mingle anonymously with the Ankave, who never know if a certain neighbor, friend, or relative may be a member of that foul brood" (Bonnemère and Lemonnier 2007: 192). They assume animal forms, especially that of fireflies, so that "any gathering of [these] leads people to suspect a band of body-eaters" (Bonnemère and Lemonnier 2007: 194).

However, it is not clear how the master-servant (human host-cannibal spirit) relation develops so that the human host has the upper hands in the relation. This is not due to possession; rather, the ethnographers write, "it is the association of a basically wicked person and a being capable of inserting objects into its victims' bodies, cutting up their intestines and, above all, affecting their circulation severing or plugging their blood vessels" (Bonnemère and Lemonnier 2007: 194). This would suggest that the "association" is due to the human person's malignancy that, so to speak, attracts and becomes the conduit for the relationship. On the other hand, people also acknowledge that the *ombi'* victims "are often people who have lacked generosity when it came to sharing" (Bonnemère and Lemonnier 2007: 196).

There is still more to this socio-moral symptomatology of Ankave *ombi'* complex. To the extent that the faces of *ombi'*-persons are virtually never visible, not even to

---

9. In this respect they echo the characteristics of Yagwoia *hyaqaye ilymane*, the wild forest spirits.

shamans (which makes it hard to make public accusations),[10] there are myths retailing encounters with *ombi'* who were recognized—not surprisingly—as *maternal* kinsmen (Bonnemère and Lemonnier 2007: 192). In what amounts to be a cosmo-ontological summation of their short account, the ethnographers say: "The *ombi'* conceal themselves inside the living; they are also figures of eternity. And if people see their maternal kinsmen in them, it is always because the *ombi'* claim they have not received enough gifts to compensate the birth of children who are one blood with them. The *ombi'* are like mothers who eat their own children, first giving life then recycling the life-giving substances by sharing out the bodies of the dead" (Bonnemère and Lemonnier 2007: 204). What is intimated here is the cannibalistic undercarriage of sociality and exchange pivoting on matrifiliation, which we saw is given an acute expression in Yagwoia kinship practices including the womba imaginary.

Given that the *ombi'* are demographically overwhelming, the foregoing also shows that the Yagwoia are correct in seeing the Yaqauwye as being womba, each and every one of them. In terms of their own self-perception, however, the Ankave differentiate between the *ombi'* and those among themselves who, so to speak, are the regular mortals but no one knows who among them may be self-conscious nefarious and willing *ombi'* hosts. Nevertheless, their own view that the *ombi'* outnumber them suggests a highly anxious intersubjectivity and world mood projection. Indeed, the ethnographers write that when an Ankave wakes up with a croaky voice, one will much more readily assume that an *ombi'* might have been cutting inside one's throat during the night rather than that it was caused by a cold. However, such a world mood may become stabilized

---

10. This occlusion of face and impossibility of identification is symptomatic of repressive dynamics at work in the configuration of the complex.

and, accordingly, suffered and varyingly tolerated, for that is the way the world is.

It is shamans who can see *ombi'*, albeit murkily, because these spirits do not show their faces, and the shamans' spirit familiars can treat the damage caused by extracting sickness-objects and mending organs. However, there were cases in the past where a dying person would name a suspected *ombi'*. They were "invariably women" who, thus identified, were either killed and thrown into the river or mutilated (Lemonnier 1998: 297). One of the effects of the government's indirect inhibition of open physical violence in their everyday affairs was that the Ankave experienced a heightened onslaught by *ombi'* in the last four decades. This situation in turn facilitated, in the late 1980s and 1990s, the emergence of a new kind of *ombi'*-finder, the so-called *bos sanguma* (cannibal-witch boss) that Lemonnier glosses as "seer." Briefly, this specialist was, so to speak, an import from the Kapau-Anga speaking area, first into the Central Ankave (Yagwoia call them Kauwyase), then into the Yaqauwye (NW Ankave) (Lemonnier 1998: 296–300). These "bosses" "detect *ombi'* inside a person's body, or they recognize *ombi'* in their dreams, and they protect the community from approaching *ombi'*. In practice, a *bos sanguma* lines people up, designates those who harbor such an evil spirit and asks them to give up their harmful doings. If there is no specific accusation, suspects are not bothered" (Lemonnier 1998: 298).

On the whole, their performance was short-lived, but their activities had different consequences in the two Ankave region. Among the Yaquwye "altogether no serious sanction was ever taken against suspected *ombi'*, at most a few small compensation payments" (Lemonnier 1998: 299). By the mid-1990s these *sanguma* finders effectively ceased their activities. Among the Central Ankave, having been identified as *ombi'* "two women were killed and mutilated in 1987 and 1990" (Lemonnier 1998: 299). Significantly, one of them was first appointed as a *bos sanguma*, her grim fate clearly indicating the ambiguity of these specialists' power of detection. It takes an *ombi'* to identify one, that is, see his/her actual face. The ethnographer writes: "Without exception, *bos sanguma* were regularly accused, in private, of being *ombi'*, too! I also heard numerous stories of *bos sanguma* accusing each other openly of being *ombi'* and then agreeing that they had abandoned their former specialty in order to become seers....As for shamans, they carefully distinguish their own ability to sense *ombi'*... from the *bos sanguma*'s power to see *ombi*'s faces and to remove human flesh from the victims" (Lemonnier 1998: 302).

One implication of these developments in the Ankave region is that the repressive dynamics of "not-seeing faces" operative in shamans and ordinary Ankave was relaxed among the "seers": one's ability to recognize the malignancy in others, it can be assumed, relates to one's own self-recognition, for the *ombi'* master-servant (human host-spirit) relationship is not involuntary (cf. Baruya shamans above). But, unlike the Yagwoia where the onus is on the person tempted by a womba to talk out in order to defuse the malignancy, in the Ankave collective (un)conscious the *ombi'* imaginary is predicated on the repression of self-other recognition. This much is suggested by the ethnographer's somewhat cryptic statement that "basically, *ombi'* have to remain unknown. On the one hand, so the Ankave say, the' *ombi'*'s origins and 'lifestyle' are those of an anonymous gang...which is obviously incompatible with a process of naming *ombi'*" (Lemonnier 1998: 301). It would appear, then, that the Ankave *ombi'* carry the burden of dissimulation of the fundamental source of the societal cannibalistic desire, which is, as their myths testify, the cannibalistic maternal core of the kinship circuit of life^death that generates and sustains their body social. This is the reason why the ethnographers surmise that "to these fundamentally ambiguous figures embodying evil and the worst side of humankind, the Ankave assign the task of representing the ultimate longevity and permanence of their society" (Bonnemère and Lemonnier 2007: 204). In the image of autoimmunity, the Ankave at once self-eat and self-preserve their body social in perpetuity.

Another implication of the Ankave development of their *ombi'* situation pertains to that idiosyncratic transfiguration within the Yagwoia womba imaginary, as it was revealed to Qang by Ma-Nguye, the Ng-Wa:ce shaman and the self-avowed leader of the local coven. He, it will be recalled, acquired his knife and third arm from the Kauwyase, that is, the Central Ankave. I am inclined to think that this is an importation and transfiguration of the short-lived *bos sanguma* specialists who were supposed to if not eradicate then reduce the numbers of *ombi'* in their midst. This is also concordant with Ma-NGuye's seemingly odd call to collectively get rid of the local womba powers, a call that to the best of my knowledge had nil effect.

The womba imaginary and the body: closure and opening

Regarding the manifestly Western hospital-morgue features figuring in Ma-NGuye's version of the Yagwoia (qua Ankave) womba imaginary, it is consonant with an established Yagwoia perception of and attitude toward Western medical practices. Most Yagwoia are mortified by the prospect of hospitalization in Lae and Goroka on the pretext that one will inevitably be operated on, that is, "cut-opened like a pig and die" in the *haus sik* (hospital). That is considered the signature mark of the White Man's medical practice. By contrast, indigenous shamanic treatments are predominantly exorcisms in the sense that they involve extraction of noxious objects from the body without cutting it open. This is attuned to the Yagwoia phallic body image whose determining feature is maximal self-closure. Over the years many Yagwoia I knew professed that they would rather die than go to hospital where a person's body is treated as if it were a pig; some of them lived up to that declaration.[11]

Yagwoia pig butchering requires meticulous cutting of the animal into a number of almost geometrically dissected rectangular pieces that are then cooked in an earth-oven. The pieces are then further sliced up into as many pieces as there are recipients. The same treatment was applied to the bodies of slain enemies in the context of exo-cannibalism. Therefore, in order to be eaten, pig (human) body has to be radically divested of its original wholeness and closure. This gustatory aspect is brought to the fore by the remarks of those Yagwoia who worked on coastal plantations and observed local culinary practices that, by and large, they stigmatize because these coastal people do not cut their pigs. Instead, the Yagwoia workers commented, the coastal people extract the innards through the anus and/or a small aperture so that the pig can then be cooked as a whole, a practice which does not square with the Yagwoia oral-gustatory sensibilities. As we saw earlier (ch. 4), the actual practice of cutting the pig and human body is manifestly a dominant aspect of the actual womba experience; this is despite the fact that the stereotyped image of womba cannibalism is one of malignant soul cutting and eating the vital organs and flesh while the victim's bodily somatic container remains intact, a feature consonant with the core aspect of shamanistic treatment of the body that involves

---

11. In the 1990s the hospital setting also began to configure the Yagwoia imaginary pertaining to the condition of the spirits of the dead. In fact, the cultural elaboration of this dimension was primarily due to the visionary experiences of shamans. However, in the dreams of some individuals during the mourning periods, the spirits of deceased relations wore white coats, suggesting the assimilation of the perceived urban hospital space into the local postmortem spirit dimension (e.g., Mimica 2006: 272–73).

the penetration into and extraction of sicknesses from the body without compromising its wholeness.

In view of all the aspects of pig = human identification detailed above, the Yagwoia perception of the way the coastal peoples treat their pigs calls for an additional reflection. How factually accurate their perception might be is an empirical issue that foregrounds the topic of the existential human = pig identification defined by the primordial modality of care (feeding) and its termination by the act of killing. This requires a paper in itself. Here I only highlight the tactfulness the Yagwoia exercise when they are about to kill a pig. By and large, it is predominantly one's ZS or/and affine (ZH, DH, ZDH) who does the slaughtering while the male owner often empathetically placates the animal that is held to know that it will be killed, that is, clubbed to death, and therefore must not be unduly upset. The onlookers are supposed to stay calm in order not to alarm the animal. This is in sharp contrast with, for instance, the Trobrianders' attitudes, exemplifying an island lifeworld, of which Malinowski gave unforgettable descriptions:

> When a pig is to be killed, which is a great culinary and festive event, it will be first carried about, and shown perhaps in one or two villages; *then roasted alive, the whole village and neighbors enjoying the spectacle and the squeals of the animal.* It is then ceremonially, and with a definite ritual, cut into pieces and distributed.
> Whoever is the master of the expedition for the time being will have brought over a couple of pigs, which will now be laid on the beach and admired by the members of the expedition. *Soon some fires are lit, and the pigs, with a long pole thrust through their tied feet, are hung upside down over the fires. A dreadful squealing fills the air and delights the hearers. After the pig has been singed to death, or rather, into insensibility, it is taken off and cut open.* (Malinowski ([1922] 1966: 171, 213; emphasis added)

I never discussed the Trobriander way of killing pigs with the Yagwoia, but I have no doubt that they would be regarded a living nightmare and "inhumanity" well in excess of, say, OMitane's nocturnal womba soul showings. Here it is fitting to be reminded of Montaigne's great insight into the source of human customs, that is, cultural reality. In his classic essay "Of Custom" he wrote: "I think that there falls into man's imagination no fantasy so wild that it does not match the example of some public practice, and for which, consequently, our reason does not find a stay and a foundation" (Montaigne 1958: 79).

Having presented the intersubjective reality of the womba complex, including its close regional affinities and variations in correlation with shamanism, I offer in the last chapter a few reflections on the rising tide of charismatic Christianity in the Papua New Guinea body social.

Concluding reflections: A new wave of Christianization

At the very beginning of this essay I mentioned the religious differentiation present among the 8 million PNG souls. Given the official self-designation of PNG as a "Christian" nation-state, I am mindful of the fact that this is a problematic state of affairs. According to the 2011 census, the vast majority of PNG's population is Christian, with Catholics and Lutherans in the lead. "Traditional" or "indigenous" beliefs are also in the mix but, as a group of "pure" practitioners, they are in the minority, together with such faiths as Baha'i, Buddhism, and Islam, and those who by self-declaration have "no religion." I will refract this official perception through the Yagwoia lifeworld, wherein for decades the following usage has had currency. Occasionally some Yagwoia individuals, when stressing their difference from those among them who are "baptized" and thereby "confirmed" Christians, point out that Christianity and the *mBuka Baibol* (Bible Book) "belong to another man," thus that it was brought in by White outsiders (*ulyce mateaqwa*) who do not have the bone and an umbilical name in the local navel of the world-body. Yagwoia thereby assert the locally ubiquitous fact that they are the people of *qwace tapatanye te* ("of this very-ground here") whose ancestral bone and the blood-umbilical names are in their territory where the navel of the world-body is and where the sky-post that holds the sky and earth in conjunction is located. Their bodily substantiality (microcosmos) and speech-language (*ququne*) are also "of the local ground" (i.e., of the world-body substance and its qualities). That is, they are literally autochthonous and consubstantial with the elemental constituents of their local lifeworld; this is the source of everything that they are as well as of everything else in the wide world as they know it. Some of them may even refer to themselves, tongue-in-cheek, as "*haiden*," a vernacularized Tok Pisin variant of "heathen." The usage carries no self-deprecatory gravity and does not mean that they experience themselves as "heathens" or that that would be their salient self-identification.

Furthermore, conterminous with their ego-cosmo-centric self-understanding is the view that the White Man's ancestor also originated in the local navel of the Yagwoia cosmic body but that he departed from the source while it was still self-enclosed, before the sky and earth went asunder. Their descendants, in the form of Australian patrol officers as the original incarnation of the "*gavman*" (government, i.e., state), reappeared in this territory because they wanted to know their source. In this regard, the Christian *nGotoqwa* (God) has been all along the Yagwoia ouroboric androgyne Imacoqwa, which is the common euphemistic name for the Cosmic Self. In general, Christian or not, most Yagwoia use primarily this name to refer to their Imacoqwa and/or the God from "another man's book."[1]

---

1. Accordingly, what is the referential and experiential reality of Imacoqwa for any of them is a matter for empirical psychoanalytic investigation since, as it is commonly the case, what a person entertains in wakeful self-consciousness does not coincide with other productions of his/her, especially the dreaming soul. I discuss this and all other variants of Yagwoia assimilation of the White Man's impact on their lifeworld and their sense of their Cosmic Self, including its metamorphosis in relation to Christianity, in another study.

A Melanesian *berit* (covenant)

The Christianized Yagwoia, baptized or otherwise, are also of the "local soil substance" except they decided, for whatever reasons, to follow "another man's book." Such a decision may not be of the "either/or" kind and, also, can be subject to reversal so that, after a period of Christian self-pursuit, a person may decide to give it up and live as she/he has been all along—a person "of this earth-place-here." This is also the case with those who in recent time succumbed to the lures of charismatic "revivalist" Christian evangelists. Baptized or not, the Yagwoia sense of self remains anchored in their authentic and local cosmo-ontological reality. This and other culturally distinctive forms of personhood and self-world relationship were not factored in when the PNG constitution was written in 1975, nor, to the best of my knowledge, when the Father of the Country, the Grand Chief Right Honorable Sir Michael T. Somare, himself a Roman Catholic, on August 26, 2007, signed a "'New Covenant' … between the God of Israel, Father, Son and the Holy Spirit and the People of Papua New Guinea" (Eves et al. 2014: 10). According to PNG's Catholic Bishops, this Melanesian *berit* states "that God's promises would be fulfilled for the people of PNG. This statement can be understood as reaffirming that PNG is a 'Christian country,' that Christianity is rooted in God's revelation to the people of Israel and that the 'God of Israel' is now for Christians 'the God and Father of our Lord Jesus Christ' (Col. 1:3)."[2]

---

2. The same source continues: "It was only later that the anniversary of the signing of this statement was declared an annual National Day of Prayer and Repentance. More recently this 'Covenant' and this holiday have been used to promote a so-called 'cleansing' of Parliament House including the destruction of traditional PNG carvings and the placement of the King James Bible in Parliament. This year, sometimes parallels have been drawn between PNG's 40th anniversary of independence and the entrance of the people of Israel into

In view of such state-managed pan-national dealings and relations with the God from "another man's book," one may question the substance of official statistics concerning how many PNG individuals do in fact regard themselves as "Christians" or "citizen subjects," simply because they were born and live in the sovereign Christian nation of PNG whose "Grand Chief" signed a "new covenant." In fact, many Papua New Guineans are anything but enthusiastic followers of this "Grand Chief" who is also the richest man in the country.[3] On the other hand, a genuine matter for empirical ethnographic investigation is how and in what experiential way this God from "another man's book" "reveals Himself," that is, becomes experienced and assimilated by concrete individuals and groups in specific New Guinea lifeworlds and their cultural imaginaries. Correlative with this fundamental aspect of indigenous dealings with Christianization is also an empirical-ethnographic issue: what is the condition of the souls of so many individuals in so far as they have accepted "another man's book" as their own, have been baptized, and live some semblance of Christian ways relative to their local lifeworld conditions, denominational affiliations, and concrete life circumstances? It is this aspect of New Guinea Christianity that I find most intriguing, especially since there has been an alarming growth in witchcraft and sorcery in the PNG body social, producing in the process such novel features as public torture and violent executions. Historically, the same sort of practices reached epidemic proportions among European Christians of the early modern period (ca. 1450–1750), marked by ecclesiastic imprimatur and extensive theological elaboration, and where the accused were dealt with in the courts of law. The number of people executed in

the 'promised land' after 40 years in the desert" (Catholic Bishops of PNG/SI 2015).

3. The nine richest people in PNG as identified by Forbes for 2018 and 2019 are or were all members of parliament.

this period, according to the most recent estimates, ranges from 40,000 to 60,000.[4]

---

4. In this regard to these figures, there was no shortage of exaggeration among twentieth-century historians, some proposing that the victims of the persecutions exceeded one hundred thousand. This has very much to do with the legacy of holocaust and genocide in the twentieth century, which some feminist scholars have used as vehicle for framing the witch-craze as "gynocide." The misogynist aspect of the European witch-craze is ubiquitous (see, for example, a psychoanalytic study by Heinemann [2000]; see, in comparison, the study by Roper [2004], a psychoanalytically informed historian). Although the "gyno-cidal" amplification is not off the mark, it also reflects the fact that the very nature of the subject matter would affect the scholarly interpretations of the European "witch-craze," so that these also articulate the present-day gender-motivated accusatory/persecutory propensities of the interpreters' (academic good citizens) (un)consciousness. For a recent treatment of these biases focusing specifically on "male witches" in the "witch-craze" period, see Apps and Gow (2003). Another important, extensive work, informed by anthropological writings, is by Clark (1997). The scholarly interest in European witchcraft and demonology has been anything but in decline, as seen in the example of just one single author, the American historian Levack. Here just some pointers to his work: his 1987 book *The Witch-Hunt in Early Modern Europe* went into a fourth edition in 2015; a 12-volume edited anthology of "articles on witchcraft, magic and demonology" appeared in 1992; in 2001 he edited six volumes on the same trinity of topics; this was followed in 2013 by *The Oxford Handbook of Witchcraft in Early Modern Europe and Colonial America* and a monograph on the possession and exorcism in the Christian West (Levack [1987] 2015, 1992, 2001, 2013b, 2013a). And in 2004 (with a second edition in 2015), he published *The Witchcraft Sourcebook*, which supplements Kors and Peters' (2000) classic "documentary history" of European witchcraft (an expanded second edition that extended the first edition's focus on

In the spectrum of PNG's current predicament and its pre- and post-*berit* trials and tribulations, the Christian evangelical-charismatic theatrics are particularly vocal.[5] For instance, on August 6, 2015, the Church of Nazarene held a pan-national meeting in Port Moresby. Following the summit, all of the more than 600 gathered pastors

> sang and marched to the Parliament House with their provincial flags. Although parliament was not in session, the pastors assembled on the steps of the parliament building and Yambe Sike, the National Board Chairman, led the more than 600 pastors in fervent prayer proclaiming the Lordship of Jesus Christ over the Nation. Then all those present filed into the public galleries and filled them to overflowing. They were given a brief guided tour of the legislative chamber by the official guide...indication is that he himself is a keen evangelical.
>
> "I believe that this is God's timing to bring you here to our parliament today. We want you to pray for God's blessing on the country," said the guide leading the pastors.
>
> The chamber of the house reverberated with the heartfelt cries of God's people as they joined hands right across the public galleries as a sign of unity and poured out their hearts to God. All those present interceded for the nation, that righteousness would be exalted and

---

the period of 1200–1700 AD to that of 400–1700 AD). It would appear then that in the megapolitan West the Devil and his emissaries definitely hold captive scholars and an educated public alike, not to mention those untold numbers whose souls are in the throes of these powers integral to the Christian cosmology.

5. For a general survey of the Christian theatrics that are staged by PNG politicians, parliamentarians, and leaders, see Gibbs (2005).

that all evil, bribery and corruption would be rejected and cleansed from the nation's leadership and that God would grant wisdom to the leaders of the nation. (Bartle 2015)

Reflecting on the currently growing influence of evangelical groups in the PNG body social at large and its political elite in particular, it is worth recalling what Narokobi ([1980] 1983: 4) wrote some forty years ago, attesting to his identity and self-consciousness as a man rooted in the earth not created by a god "from another man's book": "Our countries have been invaded by a huge tidal wave from the West, in the form of colonization and Christianization. Like any tidal wave, the West came mercilessly, with all the forces and power, toppling over our earth, destroying our treasures, depositing some rich soil but also leaving behind much rubbish."

Irrespective of the ideological motives of the work as a whole, one can take advantage of the main metaphors and ponder the present PNG situation by deliberating on how much of what is happening in respect of the state-church partnership in, and the management of Christianization of, the nation is the after-growth issuing from the "rich soil" or from the "much rubbish" that the "tidal wave" visited and revisited upon the Melanesian shores. I for one like to sieve not just through the entire deposit, barely 150 years old, but with a focus on especially such New Guinea lifeworlds as that of the Yagwoia wherein the state, only a recent arrival (November 1950), has always been and is bound to remain an ambiguously external and tentative formation brought in by the said "tidal wave" (i.e., the capitalist world system). I have no doubt that if the PNG state collapses tomorrow, the Yagwoia and similar lifeworlds will carry on being themselves, no matter what new hardships such an eventuality would deliver, somewhat akin to those among them who, after a period of Christianization, gave it up without ceasing to be who and how they have been until their souls got affected by the God from "another man's book." The empirical problematic of the states of their souls and correlative existential modifications would still remain a relevant issue.

Metamorphosis of the *imago Dei* and the spirit of the global *Evangelion*

If one reflects on the world-historical vicissitudes and the *longue-durée* transformations of Christianity and the correlative images and conceptions of God (e.g., Armstrong 1999; Wood 2005) as well as of his other, the Devil (e.g., Jung 1956; Schärf Kluger 1967; Russell 1977, 1981, 1984, 1986), one may assume that despite the official *berit*, the current bout of violent trials and tribulations is not likely to bring about the fulfilment of His promises of salvation to the peoples of PNG.[6] However, in struggling with their

---

6. The original Old Testament image of God as Yahweh/Elohim (Block [1988] 2000; Köhler 1957; Kugel 2003; Römer 2015) became historically transformed, especially in the course of the Christian eon, to the point of present-day theological exhaustion. The symptoms of this psycho-cultural dynamics of the biblical *imago Dei* are well exemplified by the history of Christianity as a whole and, especially, in the intellectual (philosophical and theological) discourses (e.g., Gilson [1941] 1967; Collins 1960; Pittenger 1982; Taylor 2007; Herrick 2003), generated as they were and are by their total civilizational matrix and its noetic ecologies. On the other hand, in unison with the post-Second World War planetary triumph of neoliberalism, the collapse of communism, and the explosion of physical science, cosmology, and (especially digital) technology, there has been unfolding an intensifying mixture of ambiguous secularization, yearnings for spiritually meaningful ways of life, economic development, and prosperity. The motley waves of new religious movements and, in particular, the transnational spread of enthusiasm for evangelical/charismatic/Pentecostal Christianity, varyingly

present predicament and the new wave of Christianization, New Guineans may at least engender a spectrum of new divine images more genuinely attuned to the passions of their souls and thus capable of transforming their current situation from within the deep deposits of the indigenous ecologies of mind rather than turning these wholesale into demonic forces of the Evil One, which is the baseline framing by the evangelicals.

Such is my anthropological deliberation on the transformative possibilities of the indigenous psyche and mind, and their immanent energies (libido and mortido) and matrixial selfhood. But the crucial conditions for such transubstantiation, the will to authentic self-knowledge and self-recognition qua a critically mindful reappropriation of the spiritual powers that grew out of and, in turn, energized numerous ecologies of mind for the last 60,000 years in this part of the globe, are anything but available. Given the present conditions of planetary humanity dominated by the global neoliberal gospel of economic development and the correlative totalizing formation of the "One-Market-under-the God-Wealth," I doubt that in the lifeworlds of PNG a state-church-managed "therapy of desire" and the pursuit of a unified national identity-image under the banner of

---

implicated in the uninhibited hyper-valorization of worldly success and wealth (in contrast to the rising tide of Islamic militant fundamentalism championing the wrath and mercy of Allah), both attest to the fact that, contrary to the expectations of Enlightenment and scientific humanism, for a majority of human beings on this planet, the God of the religions of the book is neither dead nor effectively "deconstructed" and "(a) theologized" by the many (post)modern theological virtuosi (e.g., Marion 1991; Pattison 1996; Scharlemann and Altizer 1990; Taylor 1984). Given these dynamics of Christianity and its globalized noetic ecology, which, of course, is the matrix of the neoliberal world order (Dardot and Laval 2013), it would appear that a globally most popular divine image is that of a "God-Wealth."

Christianity can stem the gurgling bellies and appetites of the body social and thereby energize the more rational and *agape* potencies of the souls of both the leaders and of those who elect them to leadership.[7] Rather, I am inclined to view the church-state partnership and spectacles of so many hallow therapeutics, especially as fueled by the motley evangelical groups, inundated as they are with charismatic zeal, as a symptom of the pneumapathology of the very spirit of global capitalism. If not the prime mover, then it surely is the titillating material and the efficient cause of the inspirited motions that stir numerous Christian and Christianized souls and their mirror-correlatives, the demonized (hence duly Christianized) indigenous spirits and soul conditions that as yet have to be renounced, subjugated, and/or wiped out.

This was well exemplified by the action of Theo Zurenuoc, former speaker of the national parliament and a zealous evangelical Christian, who in 2013 ordered the removal of indigenous carvings from the walls of the PNG Parliament House. He proclaimed them to be "evil" and

---

7. The "vision-statement" by James Marape, a Huli from Hela province (Southern Highlands), which he gave as part of his instalment speech on his appointment as prime minister on May 30, 2019, seems to confirm this. In his final words he stated that his vision for PNG is to become "the richest, black, Christian nation on Planet Earth." Given the oil, gas, and mineral wealth of the region, especially the parts that came under the control of the Huli people in the last two decades, this may well become reality for his people, one of the largest and probably the most expansionist tribal groups in the PNG Highlands. A news report stated that Marape, finance minister in the previous government that he helped depose, "is a leader of the Huli people and he defines his life by their ancient customary code" (Armbruster 2019). Faithful to the dynamics of the segmentary democracy, he and his people are likely to fulfil his vision in a pars-pro-toto fashion for the whole of PNG and its various groups.

"ungodly," therefore the Parliament had to be cleansed of the "evil spirits" that supposedly inhabited them (see Eves et al. 2014). Back in 1975, on the eve of independence, the overt consciousness of the political elite beheld a different view of its traditions. Thus, the founding prime minister, Michael Somare, who at that point might have not yet even dreamt of entering into *berit* with the God from "another man's book," characterized the traditional art forms as "living spirits with fixed abodes." The constitutional preamble from the same period states: "We, the people of Papua New Guinea...pay homage to the memory of our ancestors... [and] acknowledge the worthy customs of and traditional wisdom of our people" (cited in Craig 2010: 20). It was in the 2007 *berit* that the Grand Chief proclaimed the change of heart or, as they say in Tok Pisin, "emi tanim bel" (he turned the belly): "I renounce the worship of all idols and all evil gods. I renounce all covenants with evil spirits and demonic powers...we acknowledge you as the only God in whom Papua New Guinea stands" (Eves et al. 2014: 7).

Reflecting on the Yagwoia situation in the current evangelical climate promoted by the PNG state-church partnership, there is a possibility that for some Yagwoia, having become cleansed and inspired by the revived power of the divine pneuma, their native womba toleration may give way to the lethal attitude that, all along, has characterized their Pataye neighbors, as some Yagwoia think, from the beginning of the world.[8]

---

8. My point concerns the impact of charismatic/Pentecostal Christianity that defines its activities as "spiritual warfare" (for a good summary of the development of this militant spreading of the "Good News" in relation to PNG, see, for example, Jorgensen 2005). The history of Christianization in the Yagwoia area, and in the Angan region at large, still dominated by the legacy of Lutheran and SDA missions, had not the sort of impact characteristic of "third way evangelism." I refer to the recent collection by Rio et al. (2017) that

Although credited to Schelling, the concept of pneumapathology became better known through the writings of Voegelin (e.g., [1968] 2007: 76). However, I use the concept with the following slant: every kind of spirit, including the spirit of the God from "another man's book" (the Holy Qur'an included), who like no other has turned the planet into His dominion, is liable to cause disparate schizoid motions in the afflicted souls, producing in the process what is known as ego-inflation. This is especially so when such souls are hell-bent on pursuing their own purity and holiness, and thus motivated to wage spiritual warfare (*jihad* included) against the impure/heathen/infidel/evil souls still under the dominion of the Angel of Darkness. The luminous souls are correspondingly immunized against the mode of self-reflection that would reveal to them that the Evil they perceive in the impure ones is vitally co-configured by the self-blinding purity of their goodness inspirited in them by the descent of the divine pneuma. There is no potentially more lethal goodness than the one administered by the people of God whose goodness is the function of the Will, Grace, and Legislative Powers of the God from "another man's book."[9]

---

indicates well the lethal potential of the good charismatic Christians whose souls have been purified by the Holy Spirit (especially the chapter by Bratrud).

9. The archetypal example is Exodus 32:26–28: "26 Then Moses stood in the gate of the camp, and said, Who is on the Lord's side? Let him come unto me. And all the sons of Levi gathered themselves together unto him. 27 And he said unto them, Thus saith the Lord God of Israel, Put every man his sword by his side, and go in and out from gate to gate throughout the camp, and slay every man his brother, and every man his companion, and every man his neighbor. 28 And the children of Levi did according to the word of Moses: and there fell of the people that day about three thousand men" (King James Version) (see also Cassuto 1997: 419–22). It is constructive to compare this instituting episode

of the Israelites' "becoming a chosen people" and receiving "His promises" with the Bhagavad gita, specifically the crucial moment of Arjuna's despondence (1:20) over the imminent slaughter of his kin and kith, and Krishna's (avatar of Vishnu) therapeutic gospel that removes the noble warrior's depression and enables him to commit himself to the slaughter. There is no need to give any specific historical examples of the pneumapathological goodness of the all-loving Christians of whichever denomination.

References

Adluri, Vishwa, ed. 2013. *Philosophy and salvation in Greek religion*. Berlin: de Gruyter.

Apps, Lara, and Andrew C. Gow. 2003. *Male witches in early modern Europe*. Manchester: Manchester University Press.

Arens, William. 1979. *The man-eating myth: Anthropology and anthropophagy*. Oxford: Oxford University Press.

Armbruster, Stefan. 2019. "Who is James Marape, 8th PM of PNG?" *SBS News*, May 31. https://www.sbs.com.au/news/who-is-james-marape-8th-pm-of-png

Armstrong, Karen. 1999. *A history of God*. London: Vintage.

Aufenanger, Heinrich. 1965. "*Kumo*, the deadly witchcraft in the central highlands of New Guinea." *Asian Folklore Studies* 24 (1): 103–15.

Bartle, Neville. 2005. *Death, witchcraft, and the spirit world in the highlands of Papua New Guinea: Developing a contextual theology in Melanesia*. Goroka: Melanesian Institute.

———. 2015. "Six hundred pastors and church leaders gather together in Papua New Guinea!" Church of the Nazarene Asia-Pacific Region, August 14. https://asiapacificnazarene.org/six-hundred-pastors-and-church-leaders-gather-together-in-papua-new-guinea/

Bateson, Gregory. 1973. *Steps to an ecology of mind*. New York: Paladin.

Beaud, Michel. 1993. *Socialism in the crucible of history*. Atlantic Highlands: Humanities Press.

———. 2001. *A history of capitalism 1500–2000.* New ed. New York: Monthly Review Press.

Bellah, Robert N., and Hans Joas, eds. 2012. *The axial age and its consequences.* Cambridge, MA: Belknap Press.

Bloch, Dorothy. 1978. *"So the witch won't eat me": Fantasy and the child's fear of infanticide.* Northvale: Jason Aronson.

Block, Daniel I. (1988) 2000. *The gods of the nations: Studies in ancient Near Eastern national theology.* Second ed. Grand Rapids: Baker Academic.

Bloulet, Brian W. 2001. *Geopolitics and globalization in the twentieth century.* London: Reaktion Books.

Bohannan, Paul. (1957) 1968. *Justice and judgement among the Tiv.* Oxford: Oxford University Press.

Bonnemère, Pascale. 2016. "Church presence and gender relations in the Wonenara valley (Eastern Highlands province, Papua New Guinea)." *Australian Journal of Anthropology* 27 (2): 206–25.

———. 2018. *Acting for others: Relational transformations in Papua New Guinea.* Translated by Nora Scott. Chicago: HAU Books.

———, and Pierre Lemonnier. 2007. *Les tambours de l'oubli: La vie ordinaire et cérémonielle d'un people forestier de Papouasie/ Drumming to forget: Ordinary life and ceremonies among a Papua New Guinea group of forest-dwellers.* Paris: Musée de Quai Branly.

Braudel, Fernand. 1983–92. *Civilization and capitalism 15th–18th century.* 3 vols. London: Fontana.

Brown, Paula. 1977. "*Kumo* witchcraft at Mintima, Chimbu province, Papua New Guinea." *Oceania* 48 (1): 26–29.

Cassuto, Umberto. (1967) 1997. *A commentary on the book of Exodus.* Translated by Israel Abrahams. Jerusalem: Magnes Press.

Catholic Bishops of PNG/SI (Papua New Guinea and Solomon Islands). 2015. "The Covenant with Israel: Pastoral Letter of the Catholic Bishops of PNG/SI." Catholic

Reporter PNG, November 30. https://www.facebook.com/page/261043147262814/search/?q=This%20statement%20can%20be%20understood%20as%20reaffirming%20that%20PNG%20

Chandler, Jo. 2013. "It's 2013, and they're burning 'witches.'" *Global Mail*, February 15.

Clark, Stuart. 1997. *Thinking with demons: The idea of witchcraft in early modern Europe*. Oxford: Oxford University Press.

Collins, James. 1960. *God in modern philosophy*. London: Routledge and Kegan Paul.

Conrad, Joseph. (1902) 1973. *Heart of darkness*. Harmondsworth: Penguin Books.

Craig, Barry, ed. 2010. *Living spirits with fixed abodes: The masterpieces of the Papua New Guinea National Museum and Art Gallery*. Belair: Crawford House.

Dardot, Pierre, and Christian Laval. 2013. *The new way of the world: On neoliberal society*. Translated by Gregory Elliott. London: Verso.

Dinnen, Sinclair. 2001. *Law and order in a weak state: Crime and politics in Papua New Guinea*. Honolulu: University of Hawai'i Press.

Dupeyrat, André. 1954. *Mitsinari: Twenty-one years among the Papuans*. London: Staples Press.

Eisenstadt, Shmuel N. ed. 1986. *The origins and diversity of axial civilizations*. Albany: State University of New York Press.

Elkaisy-Friemuth, Maha, and John M. Dillon, eds. 2009. *The afterlife of the platonic soul: Reflections of platonic psychology in the monotheistic religions*. Leiden: Brill.

Elkin, Adolphus P. 1964. *The Australian Aborigines*. New York: Doubleday in co-operation with the American Museum of Natural History.

Ernst, Thomas M. 1999. "Onabasulu cannibalism and the moral agents of misfortune." In *The anthropology of cannibalism*, edited by Laurence R. Goldman, 143–60. Westport, CT: Bergin and Garvey.

Eves, Richard. 1995. "Shamanism, sorcery and cannibalism: The incorporation of power in the magical cult of *Buai*." *Oceania* 65 (3): 212–33.

———, Nicole Haley, Ronald J. May, John Cox, Philip Gibbs, Francesca Merlan, and Alan Rumsey. 2014. "Purging parliament: A new Christian politics in Papua New Guinea?" State, Society and Governance in Melanesia Discussion paper 2014/1. Department of Pacific Affairs, Australian National University. http://ssgm.bellschool.anu.edu.au/sites/default/files/publications/attachments/2015-12/SSGM-DP-2014-1-Eves-et-al-ONLINE3_0.pdf

Fitzpatrick, P. 1998. "The A. P. H. Freund collection of New Guinea artefacts held by the South Australian Museum." *Records of the South Australian Museum* 31 (1): 181–214.

Flanegan, Paul. 2016. "PNG's economy is a Greek tragedy in the making." *Australian Financial Review*, January 5. https://www.afr.com/world/pacific/pngs-economy-is-a-greek-tragedy-in-the-making-20160104-glz93w

Forsyth, Miranda, and Richard Eves, eds. 2015. *Talking it through: Responses to sorcery and witchcraft beliefs and practices in Melanesia.* Canberra: Australian National University Press.

Fortes, Meyer. 1969. *Kinship and the social order: The legacy of Lewis Henry Morgan.* London: Routledge and Kegan Paul.

Frank, Andre G. 1978a. *World accumulation 1492–1789.* London: Palgrave Macmillan.

———. 1978b. *Dependent accumulation and underdevelopment.* London: Macmillan.

Franklin, Karl. 2010. "Comments on sorcery in Papua New Guinea." *GIALens* 4 (3), Graduate Institute of Applied Linguistics, Dallas International University. https://www.diu.edu/images/gialens/vol4-3/Franklin-Comments-on-Sorcery-in-PNG.pdf

Gibbs, Philip. 2005. "Political discourse and religious narratives of church and state in Papua New Guinea." State, Society, and Governance in Melanesia Working Paper 2005/1. Department of Pacific Affairs, Australian National University. http://dpa.bellschool.anu.edu.au/experts-publications/publications/1514/political-discourse-and-religious-narratives-church-and-state

———. 2012. "Engendered violence and witch-killing in Simbu." In *Engendering violence in Papua New Guinea*, edited by Margaret Jolly and Christine Stewart, with Carolyn Brewer, 107–36. Canberra: Australian National University.

———. 2015. "Practical church interventions on sorcery and witchcraft violence in the Papua New Guinea highlands." In *Talking it through: Responses to sorcery and witchcraft beliefs and practices in Melanesia*, edited by Miranda Forsythe and Richard Eves, 309–28. Canberra: Australian National University Press.

Gillison, Gillian. 1983. "Cannibalism among women in the eastern highlands of Papua New Guinea." In *The ethnography of cannibalism*, edited by Paula Brown and Donald Tuzin, 33–50. Washington, DC: Society for Psychological Anthropology.

———. 1993. *Between culture and fantasy: A New Guinea highlands mythology.* Chicago: University of Chicago Press.

———. 2007. "From cannibalism to genocide: The work of denial." *Journal of Interdisciplinary History* 37 (3): 395–414.

Gilson, Étienne. (1941) 1967. *God and philosophy.* New Haven: Yale University Press.

Glick, Leonard B. 1972. "Sangguma." In *Encyclopedia of Papua and New Guinea*, edited by Peter Ryan, 1029–30. Melbourne: Melbourne University Press.

Godelier, Maurice. 1986. *The making of great men: Male domination and power among the New Guinea Baruya.* Cambridge: Cambridge University Press.

Goldman, Laurence R. ed. 1999. *The anthropology of cannibalism.* Westport: Bergin and Garvey.

Haley, Nicole. 2009. "HIV/AIDS and witchcraft at Lake Kopigao." *Catalyst* 39 (2): 115–34.

Heimann, P. 1962. "Notes on the anal stage." *International Journal of Psycho-Analysis*, no. 43: 406–14.

Heinemann, Evelyn. 2000. *Witches: A psychoanalytic exploration of the killing of women.* London: Free Association Books.

Herdt, Gilbert H. 1981. *Guardians of the flutes: Idioms of masculinity.* New York: McGraw-Hill.

———. 1987. *Sambia: Ritual and gender in New Guinea.* New York: Harcourt, Brace Jovanovich.

Herrick, James A. 2003. *The making of the new spirituality: The eclipse of the western religious tradition.* Downers Grove: InterVarsity Press.

Hughes, Jenny R. 1985. "Chimbu worlds: Experience of continuity and change by a Papua New Guinea highland people." PhD diss., La Trobe University.

———. 1988. "Ancestors, tricksters and demons: An examination of Chimbu interaction with the invisible world." *Oceania* 59 (1): 59–74.

Hurrell, A. Lloyd. 2006. *Hurrell's way: An autobiography.* Adelaide: Crawford House.

Jaspers, Karl. 1953. *The origin and goal of history.* London: Routledge and Kegan Paul.

Jokic, Zeljko. 2015. *The living ancestors: Shamanism, cosmos, and cultural change among the Yanomami of the upper Orinoco.* New York: Berghahn.

Jorgensen, Dan. 2005. "Third wave evangelism and the politics of the global in Papua New Guinea: Spiritual warfare and the recreation of place in Telefolmin." *Oceania* 75 (4): 444–61.

———. 2014. "Preying on those close to home: Witchcraft violence in a Papua New Guinea village." *Australian Journal of Anthropology* 25 (3): 267–86.

Jung, Carl G. 1956. "An answer to Job." In *Psychology and religion.* London: Routledge and Kegan Paul.

———. (1967) 1976. *Symbols of transformation: An analysis of the prelude to a case of schizophrenia.* Princeton: Princeton University Press.

Kindleberger, Charles P. 1996. *World economic primacy: 1500–1990.* New York: Oxford University Press.

Knapp, Regina. 2017. *Culture change and ex-change: Syncretism and anti-syncretism in Bena, Eastern Highlands, Papua New Guinea.* New York: Berghahn.

Koch, Klaus-Friedrich. 1970a. "Warfare and anthropophagy in Jalé society." *Bijdragen tot de Taal-, Land- en Volkenkunde* 126 (1): 37–58.

———. 1970b. "Cannibalistic revenge in Jale warfare." *Natural History* 79 (2): 40–51.

Köhler, Ludwig. 1957. *Old Testament Theology.* London: Lutterworth Press.

Kors, Alan C., and Edward Peters, eds. (1972) 2000. *Witchcraft in Europe, 400–1700: A documentary history.* Second ed. Philadelphia: University of Pennsylvania Press.

Kugel, James L. 2003. *The God of old: Inside the lost world of the Bible.* New York: Free Press.

Landes, David S. 1998. *Wealth and poverty of nations.* London: Little, Brown.

Laycock, Donald. 1996. "Sanguma." In *Papers in Papuan linguistics no. 2*, edited by Karl Franklin, 271–81. Pacific Linguistics Series A–85. Canberra: Department of Linguistics, Australian National University.

Lemonnier, Pierre. 1998. "Showing the invisible: Violence and politics among the Ankave-Anga (Gulf province, Papua New Guinea)." In *Common worlds and single lives: constituting knowledge in Pacific societies*, edited by Verena Keck, 287–307. Oxford: Berg.

———. 2006. *Les sabbat des lucioles: Sorcellerie, chamanisme et imaginaire cannibale en Nouvelle-Guinée*. Paris: Editions Stock.

Levack, Brian P. (1987) 2015. *The witch-hunt in early modern Europe*. Fourth ed. London: Routledge.

———. ed. 1992. *Articles on witchcraft, magic, and demonology: A twelve volume anthology of scholarly articles*. New York: Garland.

———, ed. 2001. *New perspectives on witchcraft, magic, and demonology*. 6 volumes. London: Routledge.

———. (2004) 2015. *The witchcraft sourcebook*. Second ed. London: Routledge.

———. 2013a. *The devil within: Possession and exorcism in the Christian West*. New Haven: Yale University Press.

———. 2013b. *The Oxford handbook of witchcraft in early modern Europe and colonial America*. Oxford: Oxford University Press.

Lizot, Jacques. (1985) 1991. *Tales of the Yanomami: Daily life in the Venezuelan forest*. Cambridge: Cambridge University Press.

Malinowski, Bronislaw. (1922) 1966. *Argonauts of the western Pacific*. London: Routledge and Kegan Paul.

Mann, Michael. 2012. *Global empires and revolution, 1890–1945*. Vol. 3 of *The sources of social power*. Cambridge: Cambridge University Press.

———. 2013. *Globalizations, 1945–2011*. Vol. 4 of *The sources of social power*. Cambridge: Cambridge University Press.

Marano, Lou. 1985. "*Windigo* psychosis: The anatomy of an emic-etic confusion." In *The culture-bound syndromes: folk illnesses of psychiatric and anthropological interest*, edited by Ronald C. Simons and Charles C. Hughes, 411–48. Dodrecht: D. Reidel.

Marion, Jean-Luc. 1991. *God without being: Hors-texte*. Translated by Thomas A. Carlson. Chicago: University of Chicago Press.

McCallum, P. Maurice. 2006. "'Sanguma': 'Tracking down a word.'" *Catalyst* 36 (2): 183–207.

Mimica, Jadran F. 1981. "Omalyce: An ethnography of the *Ikwaye* view of the cosmos." PhD diss., Australian National University. https://doi.org/10.25911/5d74e12bdf76c

———. 1988. *Intimations of infinity: The mythopoeia of the Iqwaye counting system and number.* Oxford: Berg.

———. 1991. "The incest passions: An outline of the logic of the Iqwaye social organization." *Oceania* 62 (1): 34–58, 62 (2): 81–113.

———. 1996. "On dying and suffering in Iqwaye existence." In *Things as they are: new directions in phenomenological anthropology,* edited by Michael Jackson, 213–37. Bloomington: Indiana University Press.

———. 2003a. "The death of a strong, great, bad man: An ethnography of soul incorporation." *Oceania* 73 (4): 260–86.

———. 2003b. "Out of the depths of Saurian waters: On psycho-Bakhtinism, ethnographic countertransference, and *Naven.*" *Anthropological Notebooks* 9 (1): 5–48.

———. 2006. "Dreams, *laki,* and mourning: A psychoanalytic ethnography of the Yagwoia 'inner feminine.'" *Oceania* 76 (1): 27–60, 76 (2): 113–32, 76 (3): 265–84.

———. 2007a. "Introduction: Explorations in psychoanalytic ethnography." In *Explorations in psychoanalytic ethnography,* edited by Jadran Mimica, 1–25. New York: Berghahn.

———. 2007b "Descended from the celestial rope: from the father to the son, and from the ego to the cosmic self." In *Explorations in psychoanalytic ethnography,* edited by Jadran Mimica, 77–105. New York: Berghahn.

———. 2008a. "Mother's umbilicus and father's spirit: The dialectics of selfhood of a Yagwoia transgendered person." *Oceania* 78 (2): 168–98.

———. 2008b. "Response: dealing with the negative." In *The uses of subjective experience: proceedings of the conference 'The uses of subjective experience: a weekend of conversations between ANZSJA analysts and academics who work with Jung's ideas,'* October 20–21, 2007, *Melbourne, Australia*, edited by Amanda Dowd, Craig San Roque, and Leon Petchkovsky, 20–27. Sydney: Australian and New Zealand Society of Jungian Analysts.

————. 2008c. "Womb = tomb = house = body: Yagwoia experience of blissful self-dissolution." In *The uses of subjective experience: Proceedings of the conference 'The uses of subjective experience: a weekend of conversations between ANZSJA analysts and academics who work with Jung's ideas,' October 20–21, 2007, Melbourne, Australia*, edited by Amanda Dowd, Craig San Roque, and Leon Petchkovsky, 82–98. Sydney: Australian and New Zealand Society of Jungian Analysts.

————. 2009. "Phenomenological psychoanalysis: The epistemology of ethnographic field research." In "What is happening to epistemology," edited by Christina Toren and João de Pina-Cabra, special issue, *Social Analysis* 53 (2): 40–59.

————. 2010a. "Flying away like a bird: An instance of severance from the parental abode (Iwolaqamalycaane, Yagwoia, Papua New Guinea)." *Journal de la Société des Océanistes*, no. 130–131: 67–78.

————. 2010b. "Un/knowing and the practice of ethnography: A reflection on some Western cosmo-ontological notions and their anthropological application." *Anthropological Theory* 10 (3): 203–28.

————.2014a. "A brief psychoanalytic ethnography of speech and knowledge among the Yagwoia." In "Psychoanalytic anthropology," special issue, *Clio's Psyche* 20 (4): 427–30.

————. 2014b. "On academic Foucauldian-dramaturgy and modernity in Melanesia." *Oceania* 84 (1): 53–63, 95–98.

————. n.d. "Imacoqwa's arrow: On the bi-unity of the sun and moon among the Yagwoia of Papua New Guinea." Unpublished manuscript.

Mitchell, William E. 1975. "Culturally contrasting therapeutic systems of the West Sepik: The Lujere." In *Psychological anthropology*, edited by Thomas R. Williams, 409–39. The Hague/Paris: Mouton.

Montaigne, Michel de. 1958. *The complete essays of Montaigne.* Translated by Donald M. Frame. Stanford: Stanford University Press.

Narokobi, Bernard. (1980) 1983. *The Melanesian way.* Boroko: Institute of Papua New Guinea Studies.

Neumann, Erich. 1970. *The origin and history of consciousness.* Princeton: Princeton University Press.

Obeyesekere, Gananath. 2002. *Imagining karma: Ethical transformation in Amerindian, Buddhist, and Greek rebirth.* Berkeley: University of California Press.

———. 2005. *Cannibal talk: The man-eating myth and human sacrifice in the South Seas.* Berkeley: University of California Press.

———. 2012. *The awakened ones: Phenomenology of visionary experience.* New York: Columbia University Press.

Overing, Joanna. 1986. "Images of cannibalism, death and domination in a 'non violent' society." *Journal de la Societe des Americanistes*, no. 72: 133–56.

Pattison, George. 1996. *Agnosis: Theology in the void.* London: Macmillan Press.

Pittenger, Norman. 1982. *Picturing God.* London: SCM Press.

Poole, Fitz J. P. 1983. "Cannibals, tricksters, and witches: Anthropophagic images among Bimin-Kuskusmin." In *The ethnography of cannibalism*, edited by Paula Brown and Donald Tuzin, 6–32. Washington, DC: Society for Psychological Anthropology.

Pouwer, Jan. 1966. "Toward a configurational approach to society and culture in New Guinea." *Journal of the Polynesian Society* 75 (3): 267–86.

———. 2010. *Gender, ritual, and social formation in West Papua.* Leiden: KITLV Press.

Reay, Marie. 1962. "The sweet witchcraft of Kuma dream experience." *Mankind* 5 (11): 459–63.

———. 1976. "The politics of a witch-killing." *Oceania* 47 (1): 1–20.

Rio, Knut, Michelle MacCarthy, and Ruy Blanes, eds. 2017. *Pentecostalism and witchcraft: Spiritual warfare in Africa and Melanesia.* Cham: Palgrave Macmillan.

Róheim, Géza. 1948. "Witches of Normanby Island." *Oceania* 18 (4): 279–308.

Römer, Thomas. 2015. *The invention of God.* Cambridge, MA: Harvard University Press.

Roper, Lyndal. 2004. *Witch craze: Terror and fantasy in baroque Germany.* New Haven: Yale University Press.

Russell, Jeffrey B. 1977. *The devil: Perception of evil from antiquity to primitive Christianity.* Ithaca: Cornell University Press.

———. 1981. *Satan: The early Christian tradition.* Ithaca: Cornell University Press.

———. 1984. *Lucifer: The devil in the middle ages.* Ithaca: Cornell University Press.

———. 1986. *Mephistopheles: The devil in the modern world.* Ithaca: Cornell University Press.

Sahlins, Marshall. 2011. "What kinship is." *Journal of the Royal Anthropological Institute* 17 (1): 2–19, 17 (2): 227–42.

———. 2013. *What kinship is—and is not.* Chicago: University of Chicago Press.

Schärf Kluger, Rivkah. 1967. *Satan in the Old Testament.* Translated by Hildegard Nagel. Evanston: Northwestern University Press.

Scharlemann, Robert P., and Thomas J. J. Altizer. 1990. *Theology at the end of the century: A dialogue on the postmodern with Thomas J. J. Altizer, Mark C. Taylor, Charles E. Winquist and Robert P. Scharle.* Charlottesville: University of Virginia Press.

Schieffelin, Edward L. 1976. *The sorrow of the lonely and the burning of the dancers*. New York: St Martin's Press.

Schram, Ryan. 2010. "Witches' wealth: witchcraft, confession, and Christianity in Auhelawa, Papua New Guinea." *Journal of the Royal Anthropological Institute* 16 (4): 726–42.

Schumpeter, Joseph A. (1950) 2008. *Capitalism, socialism, and democracy*. Third ed. New York: Harper Perennial.

Seaford, Richard, ed. 2016. *Universe and inner self in early Indian and early Greek thought*. Edinburgh: Edinburgh University Press.

Steadman, Lyle. 1975. "Cannibal witches in the Hewa." *Oceania* 46 (2): 114–21.

———. 1985. "The killing of witches." *Oceania* 56 (2): 106–23.

Stephen, Michele, ed. 1987. *Sorcerer and witch in Melanesia*. Carlton: Melbourne University Press.

Strathern, Andrew. 1982. "Witchcraft, greed, cannibalism and death: Some related themes from the New Guinea highlands." In *Death and the regeneration of life*, edited by Maurice Bloch and Jonathan Parry, 111–33. Cambridge: Cambridge University Press.

———. 1994. "Between body and mind: Shamans and politics among the Anga, Baktaman and Gebusi in Papua New Guinea." *Oceania* 64 (4): 288–301.

Strathern, Marilyn. 1988. *The gender of the gift: Problems with women and problems with society in Melanesia*. Berkeley: University of California Press.

Strong, Thomas. 2017. "Becoming witches: Sight, sin, and social change in the eastern highlands of Papua New Guinea." In *Pentecostalism and witchcraft: spiritual warfare in Africa and Melanesia*, edited by Knut Rio, Michelle MacCarthy, and Ruy Blanes, 67–92. Cham: Palgrave Macmillan.

Taylor, Mark C. 1984. *Erring: A postmodern a/theology*. Chicago: University of Chicago Press.

———. 2007. *After God*. Chicago: University of Chicago Press.

Voegelin, Eric. (1968) 2007. *Science, politics, and gnosticism: Two essays.* Washington, DC: Regnery.

Warner, W. Lloyd. 1958. *A black civilization: A social study of an Australian tribe.* New York: Harper and Brothers.

Wood, Laurence W. 2005. *God and history: The dialectical tension of faith and history in modern thought.* Lexington: Emeth Press

Zocca, Franco. 2009. "Witchcraft and Christianity in Simbu province." In *Sanguma in paradise: Sorcery, witchcraft, and Christianity in Papua New Guinea,* edited by Franco Zocca, 10–54. Goroka: Melanesian Institute.

———, and Jack Urame, eds. 2008. *Sorcery, witchcraft, and Christianity in Melanesia.* Goroka: Melanesian Institute.